A future history of the 21st century

How we overcame the crisis of civilization

FEDERICO TABELLINI

To Xianghua Li

Translation: Federico Tabellini & Marcos Francisco Pérez Browne
Editing: Andy Redwood
Cover art: Kathleen Cantwell

CONTENTS

INTRODUCTION

Milan, June 2097.

During my almost five decades as a learning mentor, I've seen thousands of children and adolescents pass through the halls of the 'Nuova Torre' School in Milan. And I would be lying if I said that I hadn't noticed a change in them. The students of today are different to those I met when I first began working there. Their thoughts, worries and actions are different. The world has of course changed deeply, and my students have changed with it. Fifty years ago, the revolutions of this dying century were headline news. Later, they became a memory, and today they are historical fact. Their consequences, which we deemed remarkable at the time, are now part of the tapestry of our daily lives, and appear mundane. In the eyes of my young pupils Luca and Marta, the balance between human society and the environment is something natural, as is their active participation in the democratic life of the school and the freedom they enjoy within its bounds. For them, the green and unpolluted neighborhoods they cross on their way to school each morning, on foot or by bicycle, could not be any different. They would be shocked to discover that a mere half century ago those vast gardens and green boulevards were constantly traversed, night and day, by an endless procession of cars and trucks.

Of course, this is not new to human history. As the philosopher Enrico Fode put it, 'nothing in history is more extraordinary than the swiftness with which men become accustomed to the extraordinary'.[1] If you were to take a new-born baby and have him grow up in the United States of the 18th century, within twenty years you would have an adult who considers slavery an ordinary fact of life. And yet the same baby, growing up in the United States just two centuries later, would come to see slavery as an intolerable tyranny, despite not perceiving anything strange in trading forty to fifty hours of their time each week, for four decades or more, in exchange for a salary. However, take the very same baby and raise him in the United States of our time and you would meet an adult for whom the idea of working forty to fifty hours a week is an intolerable form of slavery.

---

1 Fode, E. *Memories of a forgotten past*, Redbridge, 2089, p. 12.

Regardless of the society they are born into, human beings perceive its customs and traditions as normal, and adopt them as their own. Slavery can thus be an acceptable institution in one period, and an unforgivable crime in another. After all, many of the factors which led our grandparents and great-grandparents to speak of 'crisis' are now seen as fundamental cornerstones of prosperity: the slowdown of economic growth, the automation of the economy, the low levels of employment and consumption. While today the lack of jobs is a blessing, yesterday it was a social tragedy. While moderate consumption is a choice today, yesterday it was synonymous with poverty.

Although it is true that people are generally a product of their time, this does not exclude the possibility that in specific historical circumstances they can find the strength and awareness needed to mold reality into something different. When a crisis endangers the foundations of the dominant social and cultural model, old certainties crumble, and a paradigm shift can occur. As we all know, this is what happened with the great crisis that afflicted human societies in the first half of the 21st century. Now that the crisis has passed and a new paradigm has formed, the world has found a new balance. I think I speak for all those old enough to remember when I say that the new balance is better than the one it replaced. This book, if nothing else, aims to be a defense of the present before history, now that the memory of the past is fading and its specter, masquerading as the future, is arrogantly re-emerging from the grave. The relative success of the neo-laborist movements in Europe, as well as their burgeoning popularity among the middle classes, are tangible evidence of this. Almost half a century ago, referring to the bloody demonstrations of Moscow in 2049, Sebastian Volkov warned that those who ignore the past run the risk of becoming its unwitting slaves.[2] Ignoring the past is to clear the way for its return from the grave; it is much better to place it under a spotlight. This is what I intend to do in these pages: to shine a small light on the past, in the hope that brighter lights will follow. This book is divided into three parts. The first part focuses on the long decades of decline around the turn of the millennium, when the late capitalist model[3] was slowly heading towards collapse. The second concerns the period that followed the collapse, and the changes that

2 Volkov, S. *The red steppes*, Chrono, 2050.

3 The expression 'late capitalism' is used here to refer to the socioeconomic and political system that was hegemonic in the period between the 1970s and the 2030s.

occurred alongside it. The third is devoted to the birth and stabilization of the civilization that emerged from those changes.

Instead of writing a book about history, I have chosen to offer a vision of history, one that will hopefully expose and make explicit the profound reasons beneath the changes. The alternative was a list of familiar events and protagonists – more impartial, perhaps, but of scarce use against the threats of the present. Between something objective yet futile and something biased but crucial, I made my choice. I take full responsibility for it.

PEAK AND DECLINE OF
LATE CAPITALISM

There was something paradoxical in the way the opulent societies of the Global North saw themselves at the turn of the century. Their behavior resembled that of a high speed racing driver overcome by the frenzy of the race, who fails to notice he has passed the finish line and continues to frantically pump the gas. At a certain point, the tires wear thin and the car loses speed. Instead of celebrating his victory, the driver starts to worry that he is not as fast as he used to be.

At the beginning of the 21st century, the global economy was much larger than it had been only fifty years before. The finishing line represented by material wealth had been crossed long before, and there were now enough resources – at least in the most developed countries – to assure a happy life, well above the poverty line, for everyone. Yet governments, the media and economists all pined for the recent past, when the economy grew steadily, and labelled theirs as a time of crisis and decline. Like the race car driver, they confused slowing down with going backwards.

The science of economics removed the notion of a finishing line from the political landscape, replacing it with the nightmarish dream of an endless growth of production and consumption. Although for a time that perpetual growth had generated an increase in human well-being, it ultimately ended up threatening its ecological and social foundations. In the northern hemisphere, the hidden face of progress was found in rising levels of social anxiety and stress,[4] while in the south the systematic over-exploitation of both natural resources and workers was an essential part of the perpetuation of that same 'progress', and its extension across the entire planet. To make matters worse, the more the economy grew, the more of an unsustainable burden it became on the ecosystems that supported it, and the more unfairly its benefits were distributed among the population.

At that point, two obstacles were preventing the driver from bringing the car to a gentle halt and enjoying the prosperity he had reached: the first concerned his determination to continue the race (socio-cultural factors), while the second had to do with the mechanics of the car (economic, institutional and political factors). To these two obstacles I dedicate the first and second chapters, respectively. However, it must be pointed out that this distinction is somewhat artificial, and in practice both obstacles were profoundly

---

4 For contemporary data on stress and social anxiety see for example Pickett, K.E. & Wilkinson, R.G. *Income equality and health: a causal review*, 2015.

interconnected. More than that, they were mutually reinforcing.

1 A CULTURE OF EXCESS

Human beings do not observe the world as it is, but rather their interpretation of the world. When they see a tree, they associate the image with many layers of meaning that derive from stored information. The 'awareness' that it is a living organism that originates from a seed and grows thanks to sunlight, water and nutrients constitutes a filter between sensation and perception. Similarly, the charm of a sunset does not stem from its intrinsic characteristics, nor the physical ability to observe it, but rather from the romantic ideal associated with the event, acquired by each individual through exposure to their peers and the culture into which they are born, and in which they are immersed. Some interpretations are simple – a tree, a sunset – while others are more complex, like those that shape a person's self-perception, or their view of the foundational elements of social life.

In the era of late capitalism, economic discourse constituted one of the main filters that colored the human interpretation of reality. It was a filter that transformed people into human resources and nature into capital, that divided individuals into 'workers' and 'consumers', that attributed countless miraculous effects to the growth of GDP.[5] At the core of this discourse were two ethics that, with the gradual marginalization of the great political and religious narratives during the second half of the 20th century, became the primary arbiters of right and wrong, equity and inequity, prosperity and poverty, good and evil. Here I label them, following the current sociological conventions, as the 'work ethic' and 'consumption ethic'.[6]

These two ethics did not emerge simultaneously; the work ethic preceded the consumption ethic by almost two centuries. The bourgeois entrepreneurs of the early days of capitalism were above all frugal individuals who considered work a noble sacrifice for the sake of a long-term future. In fact, the entire bourgeois morality was based on the idealization of work. Work elevated man, was the highest virtue, and work was what made life worth living. The outcome of work was a divine reward bestowed upon virtuous men.

---

5 The gross domestic product (GDP) was probably the most widely known economic indicator at the beginning of the century. It is a concise measure of the market value of all finished goods and services produced in a country during one year.

6 For an in-depth analysis of these two expressions, see Cooper, J. *Manual of historical sociology*, Duranti, 2088.

The glorification of work as a virtue by the European bourgeoisie – as opposed to the idleness of the aristocracy – later spread to the other social classes, and became so pervasive that it ended up at the very center of the anti-bourgeois rhetoric of socialist and communist revolutionaries. Nonetheless, it was only with the emergence of the consumption ethic in the 20th century that the economic discourse reached the culmination of its cultural dominance. With the market already extending into every area of social and private life, there was now nothing left that could not be consumed, be it a material product, a service, an experience, or even a relationship. In the first decades of the 21st century, friendships were cemented in pubs and clubs, families passed their days together in shopping centers or watching TV, and politics, deeply intertwined with the media, was almost indistinguishable from marketing.

As the pace of social life was accelerated by scientific and technological innovations, the individual perception of time became increasingly short-sighted, and the profits of work began to be traded for short-term benefits. The bourgeois ideals of sacrifice and saving were eventually set aside, but the enshrinement of work as the pinnacle of worth and value was left unaltered. The divine legitimation of work, rooted in the protestant faith, was simply replaced by an economic legitimation: now the worker was virtuous because he provided for his own personal well-being (reified in consumption), as well as for the well-being of the state (through his contribution to the national GDP).

The gradual diffusion of the ethics of work and consumption throughout all levels of society corresponded to an artificial division of people's time between work and leisure. Time, once understood as a subjective and personal experience, became on the one hand a market commodity to exchange for a salary, and on the other a container to fill to the brim with consumer goods and experiences. The ability to enjoy a time free from work and consumption, common to all pre-modern civilizations,[7] was lost. The late capitalist man, despite all the technological prostheses that allowed him to complete tasks in mere minutes which once would have demanded hours, was dominated by haste. The conquest of time by the economy had transformed each moment that was not fully occupied into an extravagance, a nonsense, a waste-of-time.

---

7 The *otium* of the ancient Romans and Greeks, the traditional meditative practices of India and the Spanish siesta are all valid examples of this 'other' time.

Even a modest reduction of work and consumption was perceived as an absolute evil – successful people were always busy, and satisfied consumers were perpetually adrift in a sea of gadgets that absorbed every last ounce of their attention. The late capitalist society held time in such poor esteem as to consider the number of *pastimes* as a measure of individual happiness and the number of *businesses* as a measure of individual success.[8] Paradoxically, 'free' time was as busy as working time.

These two ethics of work and consumption on the individual level corresponded, on the collective level, to the productivist ideology and the myth of growth. The former converted nature from a shelter into an exploitable resource; the latter removed the concept of limits from human culture and political praxis, replacing it with the idea that 'more is better', regardless of any external considerations.

The economy measured its state of health in terms of a limitless maximization of work, consumption, production and GDP. However, human well-being – both physical and mental – is the product of optimization processes whereby the contribution of material wealth and socio-relational factors is required in the *appropriate* quantity and magnitude. If lack of food brings starvation, too much food leads to obesity and discomfort. If without clothes one is forced to suffer the cold, too many clothes lead to suffocating choices and require additional space and time for their maintenance. If the absence of relationships leaves one vulnerable to solitude and isolation, too many relationships make contact with others superficial, precluding the formation of lasting bonds. If inactivity produces apathy and indolence, too much activity generates stress and impairs performance.

Failing to recognize the incompatibility of the principle of maximization with human biology and psychology, the late capitalist model created an unbridgeable chasm between theory and practice, widening the distance between the paradise that was promised and promoted by consumption[9] and the constant dissatisfaction it generated in reality.

---

8 In the United States of the early 21st century, it was common to tell someone to 'stay busy'. Being busy was a virtue and a cause for pride, regardless of the utility of the type of 'business' that was carried out.

9 Following the definition in use at the beginning of the century, here and throughout the entire first part of this volume I will utilize the term 'consumption' to refer to the totality of the goods purchased by individuals and institutions that are not used to produce other goods, and are thereby excluded from being considered as investment.

Characteristics and paradoxes of consumed well-being

Economic growth is not intrinsically positive or negative. Setting aside other factors, its true value depends entirely on the well-being it generates for people. If growth makes people happier, then it is legitimate to regard it positively. At the dawn of the 21st century, the main indices of well-being all showed that, past a certain threshold of economic development, there was barely any correlation between per capita GDP and people's happiness.[10] In countries considered to be moderately developed, such as Costa Rica, Panama and Mexico, the average levels of well-being were comparable to those of highly-developed countries such as the United States, United Kingdom or Switzerland.[11] Thus during the late capitalist era, the curve describing the relationship between well-being and per capita income resembled that shown in Figure 1.[12]

Put simply, the more incomes grew, the less well-being any additional increase generated, up to the point, at a per capita income of around $15,000, where the correlation became negligible[13] (and for some experts[14] even negative). Beyond that point, psychological and relational factors, which were already very important at lower levels of income, became the only decisive sources of people's well-being. Other factors, such as self-acceptance, a sense of belonging to a social group or community, a feeling of serving the common good, the quality and extent of family and friendship networks and the wider social and political environment, were all statistically correlated with high levels of well-being.[15]

Beyond what we could define as a threshold of 'redundant consumption',[16] an increase in consumption is objectively undesirable, and any further growth of the economy becomes essentially worthless in terms of human well-being.[17]

---

10 Jackson, T. *Prosperity without growth: foundations for the economy of tomorrow*, Routledge, 2017.

11 See the *Happy Planet Index report 2017* and the *Human Development Index report 2017*.

12 The distribution is an unscaled approximation of the data presented in Figure 4.1 of the *State of the world report 2008* (Worldwatch Institute). See also Inglehart, R. et al. 2008, Di Tella, R. & MacCulloch, R. 2010, Proto, E. & Rustichini, A. 2014.

13 Blanchflower, D.G. & Oswald, A.J. 2004. Layard, R. et al 2008. Kahleman, D. & Deaton, A. 2010. Jackson, T. 2017.

14 For instance, see Proto, E., Rustichini, A. *A reassessment of the relationship between GDP and life satisfaction*, in "PLoS ONE", 8 (2013).

15 Among the most interesting publications of the time on this point are Kasser, T. 2007 and Csikszentmihalyi, M. 2003.

16 This concept is similar to that of the 'futility limit' proposed by Herman Daly (2014). This corresponds to the point beyond which the marginal utility of production, defined in terms of well-being generated through consumption, drops to zero.

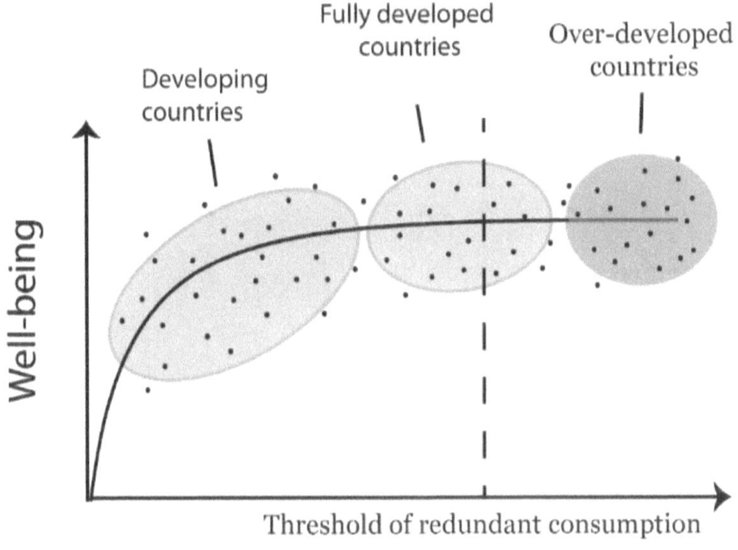

At the beginning of the 21st century, such a threshold was still below a hypothetical threshold of sustainable consumption.[18] In other words, it would have been possible to extract the maximum well-being from material consumption for the entire world population without compromising the long-term ecological foundations of the economy, assuming that consumption was shared equally among the population at the global level in the absence of overall population growth.

Unfortunately, the so-called developed countries in the late capitalist era were all well beyond the thresholds of both redundant consumption and sustainable consumption (see Figure 2).[19]

---

17 It must be noted that at the beginning of the century, consumer spending constituted about 58% of global GDP and thus represented the main engine of the world economy (data from World Bank, 2015).

18 Jackson, T. 2017. The factors that link the two thresholds will be discussed further in Chapter 2.

19 See footnote 12.

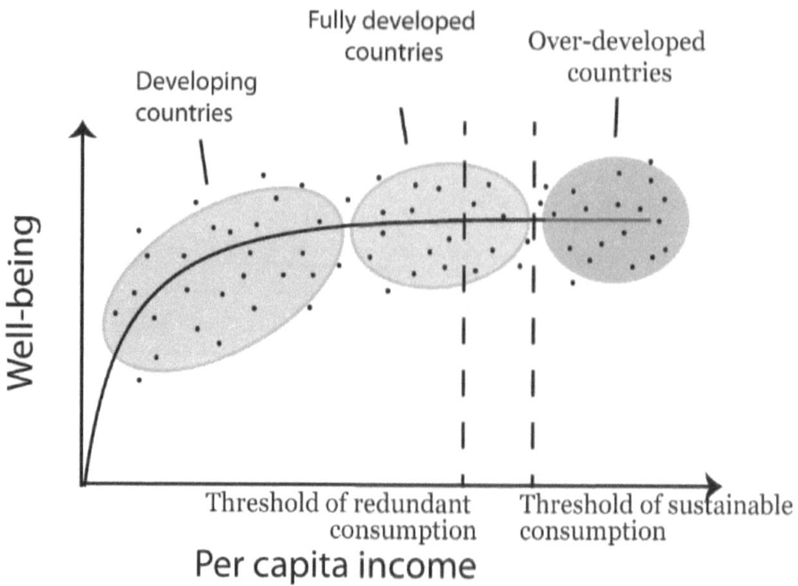

To put the problem into perspective, at the beginning of the century the OSCE countries represented about one-sixth of the world's population,[20] but accounted for about half of global energy consumption.[21] Per capita consumer spending in North America was fifty times that of sub-Saharan Africa,[22] and the per capita GDP of Luxembourg, at $109,000 in 2017, dwarfed that of Mozambique by almost one hundred times.[23] Towards the second half of the 21st century, when individual consumption eventually started to decline in over-developed countries, this did not coincide with a fall in the well-being of their populations. It did, however, free up ecological space for a growth of individual consumption in countries that still languished under the threshold of redundant consumption.[24] Unfortunately, in the early days of the new century the time was not yet ripe for such a

20 Data from OECD, 2010.

21 *International Energy Outlook 2017*, U.S.A Energy Information Administration (EIA), 2017.

22 *State of the World 2004*, Worldwatch institute, 2004.

23 Data from the International Monetary Fund, 2017.

24 See Chapter 6.

change. Not only that, but the cultural and political hegemony of economics in public discourse made whoever so much as dared to voice this possibility an object of mockery and derision.

Complicating things further, any level of consumption beyond the threshold of redundant consumption, despite being objectively undesirable, could be (and in most cases was) subjectively desired. This is because humans, far from being the rational creatures depicted by neo-classical economists, are influenced in their actions by beliefs about themselves and their social environment, which in certain historical circumstances can override any empirical or experiential evidence. Setting aside for the moment any structural considerations,[25] the answer to why consumption continued to grow during the late capitalist era, despite the absence of benefits for people, can thus be found in the enormous prescriptive power of the mainstream economic discourse. This discourse conveyed a definition of well-being that reduced it to its instrumental component, based on a series of implicit axioms regarding human nature:

- The idea that human beings are able to clearly distinguish between pleasure and sorrow, and that seeking pleasure and avoiding sorrow are the primary means by which to achieve well-being;
- The idea that pleasure primarily derives from satisfying individual needs;
- The idea that these needs are potentially unlimited, as is the pleasure that can be derived from satisfying them;
- The idea that aggregate well-being within society is simply the sum of the individual well-being of all its members.

Once the equivalence between well-being and the satisfaction of individual needs was accepted, it became quite reasonable to see an infinite source of well-being in the infinite growth of consumption aimed at satisfying those needs. Although it is relevant, the internalization of the economic interpretation of reality by individuals – by then self-identified as 'consumers' – cannot fully explain this phenomenon. We can identify at least three other key elements that

---

25 Of course, there were important economic, political and institutional reasons that made economic growth seem unavoidable, despite its increasingly tenuous link to human well-being. Chapter 2 is entirely dedicated to their analysis.

compelled individuals to increase their consumption well beyond the level at which it ceased to contribute to their well-being.

A reversal of the traditional causal relationship between needs and production. In the over-developed and over-consuming societies of the Global North, the vast majority of products were no longer fulfilling pre-existing needs – such as the need for food or shelter – but rather artificial needs, which were conveyed by the products themselves. The need to consume a 'Tasty Snack' bar did not exist before the product was introduced to the market. The system of production employed pervasive marketing and advertising to *manufacture* the needs for new products, even before they were created. The causal relationship between personal needs (excluding basic needs) and products was thus inverted, with needs springing up as a direct consequence of the introduction of new products.

A strong link between consumption and social status. A significant portion of the compulsion to consume was independent of the actual characteristics of the product consumed, but rather based upon the social significance that came along with it.[26] Even the market for individual entertainment – films, music, video games etc. – was in large part governed by logic that was unrelated to the content of the products. An essential element of this was the feeling of inclusion within a social group that came from being able to discuss these products with friends and colleagues. It must be noted that all human societies, Western or otherwise, have always placed great importance on social status. What differentiated the late capitalist societies was that material objects were the primary signifiers of a person's status. Incidentally, this fact provided fuel for the unlimited growth of the economy; if products were predominantly purchased for their intrinsic function[27] (the mobility afforded by a sports car, the connectivity provided by a smartphone), their consumption would have had clear temporal and spatial limits: owning an additional car does not make a person faster, just as having two smartphones instead of one does not make communication any easier.[28] Nonetheless, the ownership of extra

---

26 This idea was already popular in sociological writings of the early 20th century, notably those of Thorstein Veblen, reaching its most incisive expression in the work of Jean Baudrillard.

27 In modern sociology, this is defined as 'performance' (for instance, see Bloomer, J. *Microsociology for a post-consumerist society*, Phoenix Press, 2088). We will return to the concept of performance in Chapter 7, when we will talk about the transition from a consumerist culture to a culture of use.

cars or smartphones conferred greater social prestige upon their owner, regardless of their use. How much more depended on the specific social circles in which the owner moved, but in a society which had already deeply internalized the concept of a linear relationship between material wealth and well-being, and in which the rich were glorified as successful, the contribution was generally relevant.

The cult of novelty. The once-popular myth of progress (which holds that human history is a linear process in which the future is axiomatically an improved version of the past) translated into the idea that each new model of a product was evidently a better version of the one that it superseded. In a society in which the value of a product was largely a function of the social prestige associated with it, the result was that the finishing line in the race for status was constantly out of reach. Status could never be definitively gained, but had to be continually maintained by acquiring new gadgets or 'up-to-date' models of products that one already owned. The compulsive frenzy that led to the purchase of a new video game, smartphone or dress to a large extent stemmed from the internalization of an illusory relationship between age and quality. Incidentally, this relationship extended well beyond the field of material consumption, to also include aesthetic appreciation of the human body[29] and the personal relationship with knowledge.[30]

In the over-developed societies of the early 21st century, consumption, emancipated from the core functions of the products consumed, transformed them into something that was both intrinsically superfluous and socially essential. Their perceived utility went beyond the individual sphere and was largely based on the relative position of prestige that they afforded. Competition for status, accelerated and taken to extremes by the cult of novelty, was promoted and fueled by an increasingly ubiquitous and invasive marketing sector. Marketing generated a constant stream of new needs, whilst proffering the means

---

28 On the contrary, we might argue that the opposite is true. If we add the time spent on the purchase and maintenance of two cars to the time needed to move around, and divide it by the distance travelled, the result is that the more cars one owns, the lower is his or her speed. The same applies to connectivity. The phenomenon by which the over-possession and over-utilization of a type of product becomes an obstacle to the fulfilment of the need for which the product was originally designed is defined in the work of Ivan Illich as 'counter-productivity'. See Illich, I. *Tools for conviviality*, Marion Boyars Publishers, 1973.

29 In this sense, one should not be shocked by the proliferation of cosmetic surgery in the late capitalist era, to preserve the illusion of an eternally young body.

30 On the late capitalist obsession with 'lifelong learning' and the need to 'keep up with the times', a considerable number of monographs have been written. For a state-of-the-art review on the topic see Donati, E. *Time and knowledge in the 21st century*, self-published, 2093.

for their ephemeral satisfaction. In promoting new products, their material functions now faded into the background: an advert for the newly unveiled model of a car gave little idea about its speed or energy efficiency, instead focusing on the adventurous, glamorous or elegant lifestyle that it would allegedly bestow upon its new owner.

In this way, individual consumption could increase endlessly, at least in theory. Whereas the satisfaction of individual material needs has well-defined limits in space and time, the consumption of social status, ultimately grounded in the desire to be better than others, is potentially limitless. With the constant increase in average consumption among the population, more and more individual consumption was needed to acquire status and climb the social ladder, forming a vicious circle which, despite failing to generate any benefit for human beings, was essential to the limitless growth of the economy.

The consequences of consumed well-being

Contrary to the precepts of economic science, consumption continued to grow not because of its ostensible success in satisfying people's needs, but precisely because those needs, constantly stoked by advertising, could never be completely satisfied. This pushed people to constantly seek out new products, each of which would leave them unfulfilled, thereby perpetuating the system. Moreover, since the needs of the over-developed consumerist societies were to a large extent dependent on a craving for social status, the real issue at stake was not the extent and quality of consumption but the need to consume more (and to do so better) than other people. Empirical proof of this can be found in the fact that, although the correlation between subjective well-being and absolute wealth almost disappeared beyond a certain threshold, the relationship between subjective well-being and relative wealth remained.[31] People did not consider themselves happy because they were rich, but rather because they were *richer* than others. The economic filters through which society perceived reality, giving cultural weight to victory and defeat in the competition for consumption – which was paralleled, as we shall see, by competition for careers at the level of production – at least partly explained why the 'winners' tended

---

31 On the topic, see for instance Daly, H.E. *A steady-state economy*. Sustainable Development Commission, UK. 2008.

to judge themselves as happier than they really were.[32]

The relative nature of this consumed well-being contributed to the cult of maximal consumption, but it was also the principal reason underlying its paradoxical futility at the collective level. Just as the value of a sporting victory is measured by the quantity and quality of the vanquished adversaries, social status is measured in relation to those who lack it. Put another way, the recognition of a winner requires the identification of a loser. Consumed well-being, in addition to being a commodity that rapidly became obsolete, was thus by definition a scarce resource. This places it in striking contrast with both the current ideas on well-being and those of pre-utilitarian philosophical traditions, in which well-being is not merely the reward of a zero-sum game.[33] The well-being associated with the sense of belonging to a group is nourished by the well-being of each of its members, while the well-being bestowed upon the winners of the competition for reified status was fueled by inequality.[34] While the former generates social cohesion, the latter produced a superficial happiness for the winners and misery for everybody else.

While the cult of novelty made every victory temporary, the reification of social status in products that could only be obtained on the market made participation in the great economic circus mandatory for everyone. To make things worse, the competition for consumed well-being was inherently skewed: although the manufactured needs were 'democratically' distributed among the population through pervasive marketing networks, the products required to satisfy them had a price that only a few could afford to pay. The poison was free, but the antidote was not. The widespread distribution of these needs, which were inculcated into both rich and poor alike through economic and media globalization, generated a collective sense of dissatisfaction that was curable – at least, until new needs were manufactured – only for the most affluent segments of the global population. Ironically, those were precisely the segments which would benefit least from

---

32 Kahneman, D. & Deaton, A. *High income improves evaluation of life but not emotional well-being*, Proceedings of the National Academy of Sciences of the United States of America, 2010.

33 Even though contemporary economists wanted to see it as a natural fact, the reduction of well-being to its material component was in fact an extremely modern phenomenon. In almost all pre-modern cultures, both Western and non-Western, well-being was generally defined as the absence of suffering and pain (whether physical or physiological) and had little to do with the number of objects possessed or with personal wealth. On the topic, see among others Latouche, S. *L'invention de l'économie*, Albin Michel, 2005.

34 This state of affairs was reflected in the language used by advertisers. Products were often promoted as 'exclusive' and 'unique', while terms such as 'common' and 'ordinary' assumed a negative connotation and were used to refer to low-quality and generally undesirable products.

additional consumption, because they were already far beyond the threshold of superfluous consumption.[35] Therefore, while the dominant economic discourse made the goal of opulence a source of constant stress and envy for the relative poor in over-developed countries, more than three billion people (most of whom were concentrated in the least developed countries of the southern hemisphere) lived in or close to absolute poverty.[36] Sadly it was these people, who would have benefitted the most from a higher level of consumption, who lacked the means to obtain it.

The blind faith placed in the unlimited growth of the material economy was based on the idea that more is always better, and yet people in the opulent societies of the Global North were by no means becoming happier. On the contrary, their drive to feel better had transformed into the main obstacle to their feeling well,[37] a fact reflected by the growing relationship between economic wealth and social anxiety at the beginning of the 21st century.[38] By promoting competition among individuals in order to generate well-being, the economy was paradoxically damaging its psychological and social foundations. Obsessed with a definition of human well-being that was clearly contradicted by empirical data, both economists and politicians fanatically waved the flag of economic growth as if it had intrinsic value, independent from people's lives.

The ethic of pointless work

The necessary counterpart to an economy driven by the consumption of superfluous products and services – in terms of aggregate well-being – was the similarly superfluous work needed for their production, marketing and distribution. The cultural legitimation of limitless consumption through the illusion of a linear association

---

35 See Figure 2.

36 *Human Development Report 2017*, UNDP, 2017. Some of them had internalized the economic myth that consumption and well-being were the same to such an extent as to indulge in practices that bordered on madness. The members of the Sape (Société des Ambianceurs et des Personnes Elégantes) in the Democratic Republic of the Congo were poor people who saved for months or years in order to afford Western designer clothes, for the same price as a field or even a house in their own country. They would then flaunt their garments on the streets of Kinshasa and Brazzaville. What motivated them was the social prestige attached to these clothes in the collective consciousness, entirely independent of their material features.

37 The quotation is from Illich, I. 1973.

38 Pickett, E.K. & Wilkinson, R.G. *Income inequality and health: a causal review*, 2015.

with well-being made the maximization of production and employment a core element of social life. In other words, the twin ethics of consumption and work were complementary and mutually reinforcing. The equation of well-being with consumption was mirrored by an equation between success and professional advancement. Those who dedicated their lives to ascending the career ladder were rewarded with the status of successful men and women. Those who renounced the rat race or found themselves excluded from it were labelled as work-shy, good-for-nothing or simply lazy, irrespective of the reasons for their renunciation or the causes of their exclusion.

Moreover, a cultural division of time between consumption and work[39] relegated any non-economic activity to the margins. Activities such as subsistence production, DIY, volunteering, creative hobbies, housework, meditative lifestyles and political activism appeared as something residual, of secondary importance to activities performed on the market. Ironically, more often than not the former generated more well-being than the latter. Not only that, but the well-being they generated in most cases stemmed not only from the consumption of the fruits of these activities, but was also intrinsic to the activities themselves. It was not a *consumed* well-being, but rather an *experienced* well-being. The volunteer, in helping others in need, increased his own well-being in the process, whereas the marketing executive promoted vices that provided no additional well-being for themselves or their customers, in exchange for a salary that was in most cases destined to indulge in those same vices.

In order for the illusion of consumed well-being to be preserved – despite the enormous cost in terms of the human work required to sustain growing levels of consumption – work as an individual experience had to be removed from the equation of well-being. By redefining workers as 'human resources', mainstream economic discourse miraculously accomplished this removal: while downstream of consumption complex social and cultural factors were reduced to the individual dimension of consumed well-being, upstream of production human work was dehumanized and transformed into a purely economic factor, paradoxically disappearing into a collective actor – the corporation. The outcome of this was, in the political cost-benefit analysis of human well-being, the elimination of the individual

---

39 This vision also granted some marginal legitimacy to activities that were related to work, such as studying and various types of apprenticeships or internships.

time and effort of work as a cost. Per capita GDP could then appear to directly reflect the level of well-being of the population: whoever earned $1 million per year was considered well-off, whether that money was earned by painting for 20 hours a week on a tropical beach or by slaving for 60 hours a week in front of a computer screen.

Once the individual experience of work was removed from the equation of well-being, what remained was the mirage of a joyous, eternal weekend: the working man, relegated to the blind spot of the economic spotlights, magically re-emerged as a consumer in the crowded malls on Saturday afternoons. This way, even a marginal increase in well-being produced by consumption could easily appear a success, and the absence of genuine benefits from over-consumption could be seen as a small compromise to preserve the stability of the system. If a second or third car was left to rust in the garage, the only one losing out was its owner, not the workers who had spent countless hours on its design and manufacture! On the contrary, these workers had to consider themselves lucky: the rich man, through his profligacy, was 'keeping the economy going', and it was only thanks to him that they could continue to work and 'make a living'. With enough hard work and perseverance, perhaps one day they too could afford a garage in which to stash an expensive car to flaunt their own social status.

The skewing of reality caused by the work ethic and the dogma of productivism was echoed in daily language. The proliferation of useless jobs became 'employment opportunities', while sacrificing years of one's life to become more skilled in the production of superfluous goods was called 'professional growth'. Over-worked interns slaving in the belly of a big corporation were growing professionally, while street artists were bums who had failed in life. The workaholics, the up-and-comers, the priests of performance, speed, efficiency, competition: these were the role models to follow, the heroes to imitate. The widening chasm between work and the common good, concealed by an ideology that portrayed work as a virtue (regardless of its outcome) and measured success in terms of market performance, generated in workers a constant sense of anxiety and bewilderment that ironically found its main outlet in consumption. Hence the cycle was closed, and the slaves of pointless work could drown their sorrow in the same superfluous goods they had sacrificed their freedom to produce.

Even though most work was socially useless, it was not easily forsaken. A system of wealth redistribution built around the figure of the citizen-worker, which idolized him as a morally superior being, made the cost of giving up work, at least for those who lacked the capital to afford it, hardly sustainable. To this, one should add the social stigma: the young 'NEET' (Not in Education, Employment or Training) were labelled immature and irresponsible, or at the very least incompetent or lazy, whereas marketing executives and financial speculators, whose jobs were not only intrinsically useless but even harmful to society, were respected and held in high esteem. It was they, after all, who kept the economy going… towards social and ecological disaster.

Workfare and meritocracy

In the late capitalist era, any aid to the unemployed was contingent on their acquiescence to both the cult of work and the productivist ideology, which framed an individual's value in terms of their performance in the labor market. Consequently, the will to immediately enter employment, regardless of its nature, was an essential precondition for access to social aid.

Although the figure of the citizen-worker was already of fundamental importance in the classical welfare systems of the second half of the 20th century, its prominence was further elevated with the progressive shift from welfare to workfare systems at the end of the century.[40] This shift was not only dictated by financial imperatives, but also reflected two profound changes in the political and administrative culture of most Western democracies.

The first change can be understood as a gradual abandonment of any non-economic criteria in the governance of state institutions. The latter became modelled after private enterprises, wherein success was measured in terms of spending efficiency and the profits that accrued from it, and in which the 'common good' was seen as a mere by-product of skillful budget management.

The second change concerns the emergence, within public administration, of an array of discourses and practices which can collectively be grouped under the term 'meritocracy'. Here I define meritocracy as the idea, as well as the practices that derive from the

---

40 I define here 'workfare' as a type of welfare in which public aid is contingent on the willingness of the recipients to accept some kind of work proposed by the state.

idea, that allocating economic and political power to individuals based on their professional skills and academic titles would fully satisfy the principle of distributive equity. Underpinning this idea was the dubious but widespread belief that a person's academic titles and professional skills were a good indicator of their effort and motivation. In reality, almost everywhere high educational attainments and professional skills were strongly correlated with factors such as the wealth and social capital of an individual's family of origin, as well as the economic and social environment in which they grew up.[41] Given similar individual levels of effort and motivation, large differences in the likelihood of professional and economic 'success' resulted from initial inequalities in the distribution of resources. Those of modest origins – both in terms of wealth and social capital – tended to obtain inferior qualifications and salaries relative to people born into economically and socially advantaged families.[42]

Geographical context also played a significant role. Whether you were born in a small village in rural India or in the center of New York led to radically different educational and professional opportunities, which could hardly be compensated for by individual effort and motivation alone. Nevertheless, one did not need to cross national borders to witness both colossal head starts and giant handicaps in the meritocratic race. In the richest capitals of the Western world, those born into well-off families could afford to attend the most prestigious universities, irrespective of their efforts and talent, whereas only the 'best' among the poor could win access to scarce scholarships and paid internships. In other words, by discriminating according to professional performance and titles, the system was becoming perhaps more meritocratic, but by no means more equal.[43]

The rhetoric of meritocracy influenced people's psychology in subtle yet tangible ways, distorting hopes and desires. In a society where everything was considered possible for those who strove hard enough to achieve it, to be satisfied with one's position was a symptom of weakness, or even an admission of inferiority. Being gentle and happy was a modest goal – one had to be 'hungry and foolish',[44] a venture capitalist and a champion of one's time.

---

41 D'Addio, A., 2007. Karagiannaki, E., 2012. Ermisch, J. et al., 2012. Brunori, P. et al., 2013.

42 Ermisch, J. et al., 2012.

43 At the beginning of the 20th century, inequalities of opportunities were actually growing in lockstep with the burgeoning inequalities in wealth distribution, both within and between countries. This point will be explored further in Chapter 2.

44 This is a quotation from Steve Jobs (1955-2011), entrepreneur and electronics magnate.

The perception of success as something that depended solely on personal effort and motivation went hand in hand with a view of failure as the product of individual deficiencies. The poor and the jobless stopped being 'unfortunate', as they were defined in European societies at least until the end of the 19th century,[45] instead becoming losers. This had major consequences, both in terms of legislation and on the practices of social workers. Indeed, although the rhetoric of meritocracy did not alter the inherent injustice of the late capitalist distribution of opportunity, it did offer a facade of legitimacy to the perpetuation of the status quo. Just as it reassured those at the top of the economic and professional pyramids that their positions were well deserved, it also granted those who limped along its lower steps full responsibility for their own condition. By ascribing social and economic inequalities to individual differences, meritocracy transformed poverty into incompetence and wealth into merit.

Once unemployment was defined as the consequence of a personal failure, social aid by necessity took the form of a process of re-education with strong paternalistic features. Those lacking in merit did not deserve compassion, and the workfare state, when it assisted them, was always keen to make them aware that such help was undeserved. Aid was something to be earned by demonstrating a willingness to compromise. A ubiquitous precondition for the jobless to access unemployment benefits was thus the acceptance of any job that was made available to them.

Although, ironically, the economic system was largely to blame for the condition of the underprivileged, their indoctrination into economic thinking was touted with labels referencing values that flew in the face of its logic and morality. Social workers and bureaucrats blathered about 'empowering the unemployed', while politicians pompously lectured about 'lifelong learning' and 'activation policies'. Those who had been excluded from work were told that the marginal and underpaid positions made available to them constituted an 'opportunity' for personal and professional growth, a generous concession by a society concerned for their well-being. This was a lie that, paradoxically, even those who formulated it ended up believing.

---

45 Latouche, S., 2005.

Educating for conformism

As we have seen, the cultural and cognitive filter that was placed between reality and perception transfigured over-consumption into well-being, over-work into success, and economic growth into progress. Setting aside the fundamental role played by the mechanisms of social imitation, the diffusion of this cognitive filter among the population was the by-product of people's interaction with a series of social institutions, of which the education system was the most important alongside mass media and politics. Although it may seem absurd today, in late capitalist societies school was a highly standardized institution in which attendance was a mandatory commitment that lasted for many years. Notwithstanding the small differences between countries that reflected national and organizational traditions, at the beginning of the century schools across the world shared the following characteristics:

- Mandatory attendance;
- Asymmetry of power in favor of teachers over students;
- A system of punishments and incentives based on good and bad marks, praise and reproach;
- Collective, teacher-centered learning and mandatory homework;
- Standardized curricula and segmentation of human knowledge into arbitrarily separated disciplines (physics distinct from math, biology distinct from chemistry, literature distinct from history, etc.);
- A distribution of educational content over predefined and rigid intervals (academic years, terms, a fixed number of hours for each discipline) that applied to all students, irrespective of their individual abilities and needs.

It should be noted that none of these characteristics refer to the specific content of the curricula. This is because it was the organizational structure of the school, and not what was taught within its walls, that made it such an effective means of socializing individuals to the twin ethics of work and consumption.

The asymmetry of power between teachers and students reflected the hierarchical nature of the labor market. The submission of students to the teacher's authority prevented a free exchange of ideas and the development of critical thinking, making the formation of a relationship of trust between the two impossible. The teacher's role was to control students more than help them to learn; lessons were to be absorbed, rather than understood; and homework was to be evaluated, rather than corrected. The obligation to study within the confines of the curriculum, over which the students had no control, discouraged individual research and led to a standardization of knowledge among the youth. The successful students were like sponges that absorbed everything the teacher threw at them, obeying their function without asking questions, their attention never wavering from the program. Those who wished to study topics unrelated to the official curricula, or even to simply probe deeper into the sanctioned subjects, were not rewarded for their efforts. The tests the students were required to take measured little more than their conformism to a pre-packaged body of knowledge. Worse, they established a system of incentives and disincentives that minimized any deviance from the official program. The result was that students studied to pass tests, rather than to learn.

Such a system instilled in children and young people an instrumental and teleological vision of success, which was defined by something external, separate and independent from the learning process and the content of the programs. At the core of the system was not the acquisition of knowledge, but rather the mark gained by passing the tests. This reflected the utilitarian mentality in the labor market, in which workers were motivated not by the contributions of their work to the common good but rather by the consumption and social status granted by career advancement. The students who adopted this utilitarian mentality, apart from being rewarded with good marks and praise, internalized a value system that was essential for success in the socioeconomic environment in which they would operate after graduation.

Continuous testing and evaluations generated an environment of constant competition among students. The marks, often public, upheld a success ranking whose symbolic relevance was amplified by a culture that identified 'good marks' with virtues such as self-discipline, intelligence and talent, and 'bad marks' with deficiencies such as laziness, stupidity and ignorance. Students who attained low marks were labelled as losers, or at best rebels. While the competition for good marks in school served as a boot camp for the competition for prestige they would face within the labor market, it also produced an atmosphere of constant anxiety in which the pleasure of learning was lost.

As a result of the collective nature of teaching, a positive mark in the individual tests was not essential to progress to more advanced topics; that progression was instead granted to every student, regardless of their results or the knowledge they had acquired. If this progression was halted, it was solely at the end of a term, or year, and only if the *average* test score of the student was considered inadequate. Today it seems self-evidently absurd to expect anyone to understand logarithms without having internalized basic arithmetic. And yet this is exactly what the education system of the time demanded of its students. Nobody was allowed to pause. Individual assisted study, which is the norm today,[46] was not an option. Instead of helping those who lagged behind, the system labelled them as bad learners. Collective teaching not only made life impossible for slow students, it also slowed the progression of the most brilliant, forcing them to follow a predetermined pace. Neither the personal needs nor the individual capabilities of the students were taken into consideration by those who decided the content of the curricula.

The rigid compartmentalization of the curriculum went hand in hand with a similarly rigid compartmentalization of knowledge. Literature was separated from history, physics from math, biology from chemistry. The various disciplines were then juxtaposed into an arbitrary progression that saw the Middle Ages coupled with linear equations and Gothic architecture with exponentiation. There was little freedom to examine a topic in depth if it wasn't already part of the program, or to devote more hours to one discipline than another. For instance, a student could not choose to reduce her hours studying math, at which she happened to excel, to compensate for her difficulties with history. Although this may appear to be a poorly designed system to convey knowledge – and it was – its true effectiveness becomes immediately apparent once one understands that its real function was the creation of a collective mindset. This mindset exalted 'virtues' that were central to the economic system, such as industriousness, obedience and efficiency in completing highly specialized tasks, while at the same time denigrating 'vices' such as critical thinking, individual research and personal initiative. A key

---

46 See Chapter 4.

indicator of how extended this mindset had become was the fact that the structural issues discussed above were always ignored in the unruly public debates that surrounded the continual reforms of the education system. Thousands of students flooded the streets at regular intervals to protest the latest change in wallpaper, without realizing the entire building ought to be demolished.

As McLuhan wrote in the 1960s,[47] the medium *is* the message, and the scholastic medium was comprised of periodic tests, continuous evaluations, constant competition, inflexible schedules, an arbitrary compartmentalization of knowledge and a hierarchical relationship between students and teachers. It mattered not whether the lesson concerned the ideas of Aristotle or Ronald Reagan, as the study of both was driven by an external objective – achieving a good mark in the test to avoid the stigma of failure. Beyond the empty rhetoric of politicians and the media, the primary outcome of schooling was the creation of diligent devotees to useless work, anxious consumers of social status, disciplined worshippers of a purposeless growth.

If school inoculated young people with the twin ethics of work and consumption in order to cultivate a collective delusion of the merits of the late capitalist model, then universities provided the conditions for that model to flourish. During the 20th century, universities gradually metamorphosed from bastions of knowledge into factories that churned out human resources, career workshops in the service of the economic system. By the turn of the century the transformation was complete, and the universities themselves promoted their courses as springboards for specific careers. In advertising a medicine degree, the promised outcome was not 'the acquisition of skills for curing the sick', but rather 'professional opportunities in private and public clinics'. That this appeared entirely natural to both students and the university staff speaks volumes about how deeply rooted the ethic of work and the productivist ideology were in the late capitalist zeitgeist.

Universities no longer trained young people to be intellectuals, but instead molded them to serve as hyper-specialized technicians versed in a minuscule niche of knowledge, efficient gears in an economic machine hurtling at high speed towards social and ecological suicide. These people obtained social prestige and economic clout by sacrificing the search for holistic knowledge in favor of developing an instrumental know-how. Bereft of any non-economic point of

---

47 McLuhan, M. *Understanding media: the extensions of man*, Signet Books, 1966.

---

reference or bigger picture, the children of this dehumanized progress were sucked into the maelstrom of careers and consumption and lived their lives between the office and the shopping center. The economic filter on reality convinced them they were living life in the right way, blinding them to the consequences of their actions. The marketing expert was not responsible for the plastic choking the oceans, and nor were the people who produced and consumed it. This shared responsibility belonged to everyone, and therefore no one; or perhaps it belonged to politicians, who were assigned the impossible task of solving problems without jeopardizing the growth of production, employment rates and levels of consumption. In other words, through some kind of magic or miracle.

Mandatory and standardized schooling had transformed the youth into an army of conformists educated into a teleological and instrumental perspective of life. Universities had molded them into useful gears to turn the wheel of growth. In this sense, the education system created learned people in the same way as consumption created well-off people and work created successful people. The number of schools in a country could then reflect the level of education of its population, the way per capita GDP reflected its well-being.

A colonized land

The influence of the economic model predicated on unlimited growth was so pervasive that its influence even extended to spatial planning. The late capitalist city, which at the beginning of the century was home to more than half of the world's population, was a dissipative system[48] that consumed lands ever farther from its center, devouring them with its incessant expansion. Theoretically, by simplifying the transportation of energy and goods, the concentration of millions of individuals in a single place should have reduced the population's aggregated ecological impact. Instead, it increased it exponentially.[49] Geographical proximity made the competition for

---

48 A dissipative system is a thermodynamically open system which exists in a non-equilibrium state with respect to its environment, preserving its stability only due to a continuous absorption of energy and matter from its surroundings. The term was originally coined by the Nobel Prize winner Ilya Prigogine in the 1960s.

49 Magnaghi, A. *Il progetto locale. Verso la coscienza di luogo*, Bollati Boringhieri, 2010. The topic of the ecological unsustainability of the late capitalist model will be thoroughly discussed in the next chapter.

commodified status even fiercer and, together with the greater exposure of city-dwellers to media and advertising, inevitably raised the levels of individual consumption. At the beginning of the 21st century, the city of London alone – not an exception among the other late capitalist metropolises – consumed resources equal to those produced by the entirety of England.[50]

With the progressive concentration of the principal economic, political and administrative functions in the cities, the remaining land was converted from a heterogeneous melting pot of living *places* into a mere *space*, where economic and productive units (the residential and agricultural estates, the industrial areas, the tourist villages, the dumps) were scattered indiscriminately. In the new core-periphery model, the complex environmental, historical, artistic, architectural and cultural heritage that had once characterized the land was gradually replaced by a compartmentalized void to be crossed at high speed in order to reach the core urban hubs or, when profitable, to be packaged and transformed into a tourist product for mass consumption.

The cities themselves, mass-produced according to the principles of economic efficiency, presented the same features (building materials, architectural styles, urban organization) from Shanghai to Madrid, from Cape Town to Moscow. Their few unique characteristics – mostly vestiges of past epochs – were converted into open-air museums that painfully contrasted with their urban surroundings. Beijing's Forbidden City was shrouded in a shapeless mass of buildings that reproduced, with few variations, the grey scenery that surrounded Milan's Sforza Castle.

The spatial separation between production (relegated to peripheral areas) and consumption (concentrated within the city) generated individuals for whom products magically appeared on the supermarket shelves, and just as magically disappeared after being dumped in the trash. They were consumers of meat, fish, fruit and vegetables who had never seen farm animals, fishing boats, orchards or vegetable gardens, and were thus unable to evaluate their own ecological impact. And this was not because they actively avoided doing so, but simply because the consequence of their consumption had been relocated elsewhere, where they could not see it – to the dumps in the periphery, the factory-villages of the Global South, the ravaged oceans and forests depleted of biodiversity and resources. This new type of person

---

maintained a predatory relationship with the urban environment, and consumed places rather than dwelling in them. They conceived the public space as little more than a link between localized economic functions (the office, the restaurant, the shopping center, the gym). Their relationship with these places was almost exclusively as a worker or consumer, and they moved between them as quickly as possible, so as not to waste their perpetually scarce time.

Unfortunately for them, just as the products and services that they frantically accumulated did not increase their well-being, so the hefty cars they used to move around – all too often alone at the wheel – did not reduce the time needed for their errands. Over time, the rapid travel afforded by cars had caused the average distance between home and work to increase. This, together with the ubiquitous congestion that afflicted late capitalist cities, reduced the actual average speed of cars to the point where, as Ivan Illich had already noted in the 1970s, they were barely faster than a common bicycle.[51]

We could go on, but the central point is that the core-periphery model, not unlike the growth model, had long ago ceased to serve people's well-being, instead turning them into the unconscious gears for its self-perpetuation. Like a parasite that feasts on the host until it almost kills it, the urban sprawl fed on a territory that now extended to the entire planet, reducing it little by little to a uniform expanse of grain and concrete.

---

51 Illich, I. *Energy and equity*, Harper & Row, 1974. This is even more the case if one considers not only the time spent driving the car, but also the time spent for its maintenance and the hours of work required to pay for it.

2 A SYSTEM IN CRISIS

Why did governments pursue growth at all costs when it no longer generated significant well-being for people? Why were great efforts made to maintain high levels of employment, despite the constant decline in the importance of human labor to production? Why did media pundits, economists and politicians insist that consumption had to grow, in spite of its environmental unsustainability and its blatant failure to make individuals happier?

In Chapter 1 we provided only a partial answer to these questions, focusing on the core cultural and social factors that characterized the late capitalist model. In this chapter, we will explore its structural factors – economic, financial, institutional and political – to try to reach a more complete answer.

The smuggled wealth

The only thing worse than love of money as an evil that is *necessary*, in a society that needs more growth and production for its survival, is love of money as an *unnecessary* evil, in an over-developed society that is drowning in superfluous goods. It is well established that, at the dawn of the century, human civilization had reached a level of material production sufficient to guarantee a comfortable life to the entire global population. During the 20th century, the production of grain per hectare increased fourfold. Similar spikes in efficiency were the norm in both agriculture and industry. In real terms, the global GDP in the year 2010 was eight times that of 1950. Over the same period of time, the global population grew 'only' threefold. Likewise, we know that the growth of material production went hand in hand with an increasingly skewed distribution of wealth. By the end of the second decade of the 21st century, the richest 1% of the global population possessed as much wealth as the remaining 99%. Just eight billionaires controlled a fortune equal to that of the poorest 50% (some 3.6 billion people),[52] of whom 800 million went hungry. It is estimated that $100 billion, equivalent to

---

52 *An economy for the 99%*, Oxfam, 2017.

0.01% of global GDP at the time, would have been sufficient to feed them all.[53] Incidentally, this was about 20% of the money spent annually on marketing worldwide.[54]

It is clear that the capitalist system, despite its undeniable efficiency at generating an unprecedented level of material wealth, was utterly inefficient when it came to its distribution. Far from furthering the common good, the once-glorified invisible hand of the market proved to be a sort of evil Robin Hood, stealing from the poor to give to the rich – so much so that the prosperity created by growth, instead of 'trickling down', was 'sucked up' at an accelerating rate.

The yawning gulf between the rich and the poor, whose profound causes we will explore in the following pages, tended to widen due to a complex feedback loop by which the more capital one controlled, the easier it became to accumulate still more. First of all, the most prominent tycoons had access to managerial and administrative means unavailable to the masses. With their wealth, they could afford the best financial consultants, streamline their organizations and wield unmatched technological resources. Second, by dissolving most economic borders and fostering the free movement of capital, globalization had considerably reduced state control over capital flows. If their demands were not met, large corporations and financial trusts did not hesitate to transfer their enormous resources[55] to countries with more advantageous taxes and labor costs.

The result was a ruthless race to the bottom among states striving to attract capital investment. In the United States, the tax rates on the richest segment of the population dropped from 70% in 1980 to only 40% in 2016. In the same year, the top tax rates in so-called developing countries averaged 30%.[56] This situation produced a contraction of public budgets, leading to a shrinkage of national welfare systems that was to the detriment of the lowest social classes. At the same time, it served to further concentrate wealth into the coffers of the richest 1% sitting atop the pyramid. In striking contrast with the work ethic and meritocratic rhetoric that permeated political and economic discourse, the pyramid was capped by individuals who owed their privileged position not to their work, but rather the enormous financial,

---

53 UNDP, 2017.

54 Data from the World Bank, 2017.

55 To give an idea of the size of the capital wielded by large corporations, in the year 2015 the 10 largest moved more money internationally than the combined annual budget of 180 states. Source: Oxfam Briefing Paper, January 2017.

56 *Ibid.*

technological and organizational capital they controlled. They were succeeded on the second step of the pyramid by the top managers, who handled this massive capital on their behalf. The salaries of these managers were senselessly high. At the beginning of the 1980s, the ratio of CEO earnings to the average salary of their workers was around 35:1, but by the beginning of the 21st century it had soared to 300:1.[57] On the next step of the pyramid were professionals, low-level executives and small businessmen. For reasons that will be addressed later, both the size of this sector of society – referred to at the time as the middle class – and the resources they controlled were rapidly shrinking. Finally, at the base of the pyramid were the expanding multitude of the poor, the unemployed and the precariat, a group that included the vast majority of the world's population.

Technological unemployment

Beyond the pernicious effects of specific monetary policies – which we will address shortly – the main cause of the growing economic inequalities was systemic in nature. Between the middle of the 20th century and the beginning of the 21st, technological innovation and the widespread automation of production increased the average productivity of work by around threefold,[58] reducing the number of workers required for the proper functioning of the economy.

Initially, although technology displaced human labor in many professions, the constant growth of production – fueled by over-consumption and a market for goods and services that was not yet saturated – made it possible to maintain stable levels of employment for many decades, with the exception of occasional economic recessions. However, at the dawn of the new century the situation was rapidly changing. Despite the considerable efforts expended to foment the cult of novelty and the consumption of status by increasingly aggressive and pervasive advertising, markets were approaching saturation and growth had begun to falter, at least in the over-developed economies. Conversely, technological innovation continued

---

57 Mischel, L. & David, A. *CEO pay continues to rise as typical workers are paid less*, Economic policy institute, Issue brief n. 380, 2014.

58 This figure is based on the OSCE countries (plus Japan) in the period between 1950 and 2016, excluding Hungary, the Czech Republic, Estonia, Latvia and Israel. Source: *The Conference Board Total Economy Database*, The Conference Board, 2016.

to advance, replacing an ever-increasing number of workers and boosting the efficiency of those who remained, thus reducing the demand for labor. And if the heavy machinery of the first industrial revolution had mainly eliminated manual jobs, modern computers and robots came to have an impact on a much wider range of professions, including many that were intellectual and relational in nature. By taking orders through a palmtop computer, waiters eliminated the need for constant scurrying to and from the kitchen, reducing the staff required to manage each restaurant or bar; warehouse workers could take inventory of the stock of products and goods in just a few minutes thanks to sophisticated management software, making each worker worth two or three of their predecessors; teachers and professors, supported by modern e-learning platforms, could deliver online lectures to hundreds of students simultaneously, rendering many of their colleagues superfluous; a growing number of tour and museum guides in the tourism industry were replaced by constantly updated electronic guides, in most cases available for free on every tourist's smartphone. We could go on. The only jobs that somehow survived technological unemployment were those in which human empathy was a central component (caregivers, nurses, psychotherapists etc.), religious vocations (such as monks and priests) and highly creative professions (artists, managers etc.).

In addition to their high level of efficiency and low price, new technologies offered entrepreneurs several other advantages over human workers. The law granted them no rights and, unlike people, they never complained or went on strike. They worked 24 hours a day, 365 days a year. They did not get sick or fall pregnant. They took no coffee or bathroom breaks. In other words, they were the perfect workers.

The value and efficiency of new technologies relative to human workers was further demonstrated by the success of the companies which used them most intensively: in the early years of this century, the fastest growing companies were almost exclusively capital-intensive. Companies such as Google, Apple, Amazon and Facebook showed profit margins that dwarfed those of traditional companies, which employed a much larger workforce. While at the beginning of the 1990s the three largest manufacturing companies had 1.2 million employees and a market capitalization of $36 billion, in 2015 the market capitalization of the three largest companies in Silicon Valley, with only 137,000 employees, was 30 times higher.[59] The reduced demand for workers by companies, in the context of a constant supply of labor, inevitably led to a contraction of salaries. The bitter irony was that the higher productivity of workers was a major cause for the reduction in their wages.

With the economic development of the Global South and the consequent rise in workers' rights and remuneration, it would not be long before many multinational corporations that had moved their manufacturing offshore began to bring their factories back home to the North. Once there, they would replace manual laborers with technology and cut staff to the small number of technicians and experts required to keep production operational. Although many economists had initially entertained the idea that these new hyper-specialized jobs could compensate for those lost to technological innovation, this notion was eventually discarded in the face of a reality that clearly disproved it.[60]

The main driving force of the economy was now capital. As the contemporary reader will surely notice, this was in fact a fortunate turn of events, as it meant that people could finally work fewer hours and devote themselves to self-chosen activities that would bring them greater well-being. The only condition necessary for such a scenario to become reality was for the profits derived from the world's technological, material and organizational capital to be equally redistributed among the population. The fact that most of this capital was inherited from the past rather than created from scratch made it by right a good whose ownership ought to be shared by all human beings. And herein lay the main problem: despite the clear emergence of a post-work economy, both the fiscal and redistributive systems were still dependent on work. This was so much the case that with every dip in employment levels, there was a corresponding reduction in public spending[61] and a sudden mass of unemployed people who lacked any form of income.

In other words, from the standpoint of both material production and human well-being, there was far too much work, while from an economic and institutional standpoint there was never enough. As we

---

59 Frey, C.B., Osborne, M. *Technology at work. The future of innovation and unemployment*, University of Oxford, 2016.

60 At the beginning of the 2010s even economists at MIT had to admit the existence of a correlation between technological innovation and unemployment. See Brynjolfsson, E. & McAfee, A. *Race against the machine: how the digital revolution is accelerating innovation, driving productivity and irreversibly transforming employment and the economy*, Digital Frontier Press, 2011.

61 This reduction in public spending could be avoided by increasing public debt, but the overall result of this would only be to postpone, and often ultimately aggravate, the effects of the underlying problem.

all know, instead of following the logical step of reforming the fiscal and redistributive systems to adapt to a post-work society, the political elite, influenced by the preaching of the economists, opted to push with renewed energy on the accelerator of growth, in a masochistic struggle against a technological revolution that could have easily freed the population from the slavery of compulsory work.

Today, in light of the profound changes that have occurred in the last few decades, it is easy to blame our ancestors for failing to become aware of and seize the opportunity within their reach for so many years. However, taking into account how deeply rooted the consumerist and productivist culture was in the heart and soul of late capitalist societies, not to mention the complex institutional networks that served to secure their perpetuation, the changes were surprisingly swift. Meanwhile, during the tumultuous decades preceding the transition, politicians and economists saw no better way but to try and solve what appeared to them as a problem by resorting to the old solutions – pushing for economic growth, in the misguided hope that this would be enough to compensate for burgeoning levels of unemployment and inequality. When the reality of technological unemployment finally became apparent, many argued that the only alternative to growth was a constant rise in unemployment, a continuous contraction of salaries and a widening of the economic and power gap between capitalists and workers. This would have naturally caused a drop in consumer spending, followed by a shrinking of corporate profits, in a recessionary spiral that would have ultimately led to a collapse of the entire economic system. Of course, such an apocalyptic scenario would have also dragged down the giant financial conglomerates, whose profits were based – whether directly or indirectly – on consumer spending. What people of the time seemed willfully ignorant of was that economic growth was not simply slowing down: it was also weakening its association with employment. Each marginal increment of global GDP produced ever-feebler boosts to employment rates,[62] making the fight against technological unemployment by means of economic growth an impossibility for the developed economies, and at best a temporary solution for developing economies.

In the meantime, while the economic growth that governments desperately grasped at was gradually losing all its historical benefits, the

---

62 De Masi, S. *Lavorare gratis, lavorare tutti. Perché il futuro è dei disoccupati*, Rizzoli, 2017.

rising tension between the unemployed and the over-employed made life miserable for both. While the former were constantly bombarded by advertisements for goods and services they could not afford, the latter were required to work and consume at a frantic pace in order to support a system that left them with just the crumbs. To complicate matters further, the division between the unemployed and the over-employed was also generational: the youth of the early 21st century – the most educated in history – could not find employment, while their parents worked themselves to death to protect their little privileges. An entire generation was thus left to fend for itself in the limbo between a work-based society in terminal decline and a post-work society that had yet to be born.

Ironically, the fewer workers the system required, the more the universities embraced the work ethic. Politicians, economists and the media all called on young people to study disciplines 'with a future', such as math, finance or engineering – disciplines that could perhaps prove useful to further reduce the need for work in the economy, but were certainly unable to produce citizens capable of comprehending the system's contradictions and igniting sparks of change. Those who dared to study the humanities were told that if they wanted a job they should invent one for themselves, a daunting task in a nearly saturated market. The consequence was young people with one or more university degrees taking up increasingly trivial occupations, from dog sitters to personal shoppers, from social media managers to elevator operators. These same young people, if only given the opportunity, could have used their time to engage in active and useful leisure. But the twin ethics of work and consumption dictated that nothing was for free, and one had to 'make a living', as the saying went – through a job, any job, regardless of its utility.

The late capitalist economy, shored up by the over-consumption of the moribund middle class, prescribed a role for everyone as a cog in the battered mega-machine of growth, the fruits of which flowed mostly into the already stuffed pockets of the super-rich. Contrary to the hegemonic meritocratic rhetoric, these people owed their privileged position not to their talent but rather their ability to secure for themselves an outsized slice of the common heritage – of nature, technology and knowledge. The workers could thus be proud of themselves: they were spending their lives struggling in an office or factory to produce pointless gadgets, in order to access the scraps of wealth generated by the few of them still tasked with the production of useful goods and services.

Such was the situation at the dawn of the century, before cars and trucks became driverless and drones permanently replaced postmen and couriers; before call center workers were deprived of their jobs by modern artificial intelligence, and automatic translation software did away with translators and interpreters; before restaurant staff were made redundant by the diffusion of orders-by-app and robotic kitchens, and automatic shops rendered retail staff superfluous. In order to postpone the dreaded change for a few more decades, they went as far as deliberately manufacturing products that were not only utterly inessential but also purposely fragile, so that their constant need for replacement would artificially boost product sales. This phenomenon, known as planned obsolescence, was exemplified in its most extreme forms by the foolish substitution of long-lasting products with their equivalent single-use versions.

Credit, monetary expansion and the economic cycle

The next two sections of this chapter aim to clarify one of the most obscure and complex elements of this story: the fundamental role played by the financial system in the perpetuation of the late capitalist model through the long years of its decline, as well as its final collapse. As a thorough dissection of such a complex system is impossible within the limited scope of the current work, here we will limit ourselves to answering three fundamental questions:

- Why was the stability of growth economies intimately dependent upon a constant expansion of the money supply?[63]
- What measures were available to states and central banks to guarantee such an expansion?
- What negative consequences did these measures have on the late capitalist economies and societies, and why do we refer to these consequences today as a 'growth trap'?

---

63 For our present objectives, I will define the money supply simply as the sum of all the available money in the economy. This includes, among other things, money in circulation, in deposit accounts, and held as bonds or debentures.

This section will address the first two questions, while the next section will be entirely dedicated to the third.

Why was the stability of growth economies intimately dependent upon a constant expansion of the money supply?

As is well known, in any market economy in which the money supply is held stable, the growth of aggregate production leads to a general reduction of prices, referred to as *deflation.*

An example will help to clarify this concept. Let us imagine an economy in which there are only 10 pastries and 100 coins available on the market. With all else equal, the law of supply and demand will make each pastry cost exactly 10 coins. If the total quantity of pastries on the market increases to 100 units, the price of each pastry, adapting to the available money supply, would drop to just one coin each (to the delight of the sweet-toothed consumer).

In the presence of work-based redistributive and fiscal systems[64] – this was the case with late capitalist societies – deflation represents a sure-fire recipe for recession. The reason is simple. The progressive reduction in prices makes future purchases more desirable than present ones, leading to an increase in savings and a drop in consumer spending. This in turn damages private sector profits, leading to job losses. In the absence of a means for wealth redistribution other than salaries, the lower employment rates produce a further contraction of aggregate consumption, triggering a recessive spiral (see Figure 3). To make matters worse, lower employment rates translate to lower fiscal revenues, which makes it more challenging for states to adopt measures to counter the recession. This explains why deflation in growth economies was considered to be the worst of all evils. It also explains why orthodox economics (in its neo-Keynesian variant) hatched a scheme to prevent such a scenario from becoming reality.

The scheme was fairly simple: the economy had to be kept in a state of constant inflation.[65] Indeed, if prices were to rise indefinitely, present purchases would always be cheaper than future ones, thus

---

64 According to current usage in sociology, a fiscal and redistributive system is referred to as 'work-based' when wages represent both one of the main sources of public funds and the main mechanism of wealth redistribution.

65 Although the two concepts do not fully overlap, in order not to unnecessarily complicate things here and for the remainder of the book I use the term 'inflation' as synonymous with 'generalized price increases in the economy'.

providing a disincentive against saving and redirecting income towards consumer spending. With the endless growth of production that characterized the late capitalist economies, the only way to do this was through a similarly endless – though, as we are about to see, controlled – increase of the money supply. The latter would have to grow faster than aggregate production. Put another way, for each new pastry that left the oven, the central bank would have to introduce more than one coin into circulation.

<u>**Figure 3. Recessive cycle in the context of work-based redistributive and fiscal systems**</u>

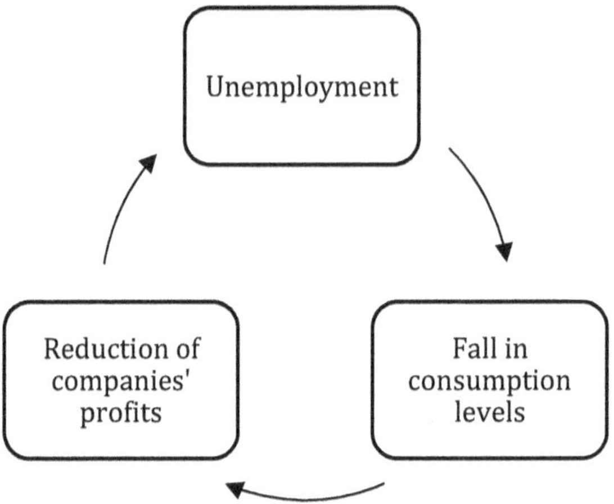

There was, however, another important reason why monetary expansion constituted a central element of the late capitalist economic model: the constant flow of new money into the economy encouraged banks to reduce interest rates on loans, stimulating more investment and consumer spending and promoting economic growth. In other words, monetary expansion was to the economy what doping was to an athlete: the economist-coach would proudly proclaim that, given the right monetary injection, growth could continue eternally, for the 'happiness' of all.

<u>What measures were available to states and central banks to guarantee a constant expansion of the money supply?</u>

States and central banks had three fundamental measures to manipulate the size of the money supply. These were:

- Adjustment of the cash reserve ratio;
- Modification of the discount rate at which the central bank lent fresh money to commercial banks;
- The sale or purchase of government bonds by the central bank (at the time known as 'open market operations').

We will examine each of these measures in turn.

Adjustment of the cash reserve ratio. Unlike today, at the turn of the century commercial banks were obliged by law to retain only a small fraction of the total balance of their client's deposits in their vaults. The remainder could be freely loaned or reinvested by the bank without the explicit consent of its owners, under the sole condition that the bank would have to return the money if the client requested it. This system, known as 'fractional reserve banking', was the consequence of the realization that, at any given moment, only a small percentage of depositors requested access to their money, making it possible for banks to satisfy the requests of all clients with only a minimal fraction of the total balance of deposits in their reserve. That fraction, established by law, was known as the 'cash reserve ratio'.

The lower the cash reserve ratio that the banks had to abide by, the more money they had available for loans to companies and private citizens. Of course, this had a direct effect on investments and consumer spending. Thus, in the course of the 20th century, central banks continuously lowered the cash reserve ratio, up to the point where, at the turn of the millennium, it had reached single digits.[66]

But how did reducing the cash reserve ratio lead to an increase in the money supply? To answer this question, we must first understand a mechanism known as the 'money multiplier'. Due to its complexity, the best way to explain its function is through a simplified scenario that, although sacrificing something in terms of analytical depth, does not differ in its basic elements from the reality of the time.

In the imaginary society of Bankland there is only one bank, and all

---

66 After 2012, in Europe the cash reserve ratio dropped to a mere 1%.

of the money available, a total of $100, is initially held by John as cash. One day John decides to put his $100 in the bank, opening a deposit account. If the bank were expected to observe a 100% cash reserve ratio, it could not lend out any of John's money. However, the laws of Bankland stipulate that the bank must observe a cash reserve ratio of only 10% of the total balance of deposits. As such, the bank is free to lend the rest of the money, a total of $90, to Albert. And here is where the problems begin. John and Albert together now have access to a total of $190, despite an initial deposit of only $100 in the bank's vaults.

Let us now imagine that Albert decides to use his $90 to buy goods from a third person, Lucy. Upon receiving payment from Albert, Lucy also deposits the money in the bank, opening a new deposit account. Respecting the obligatory cash reserve ratio of 10%, the bank decides to lend out $81 of Lucy's money to Susie, who chooses to put the entire sum in yet another deposit account.

By now, the total money available in Bankland is $271 (John's $100 + Lucy's $90 + Susie's $81), and the cycle continues until the bank lends away all the money deposited, with the exclusion of what it is mandated to keep by the cash reserve ratio. The final result is expressed by the equation $mm = 1/rr$. The money multiplier (mm) is equal to the inverse of the cash reserve ratio (rr). In our case, with a ratio of 10% (making rr = 0.1), the money supply is multiplied by a factor of 10, and the people of Bankland would eventually have access to a total of $1000 in their deposit accounts, all of it stemming from a single initial deposit of $100.[67] In such a situation, if the Banklanders all decided to withdraw as little as 10% of their savings simultaneously, the bank would be forced to declare bankruptcy.

This is in essence how the banking system worked in the late capitalist societies, with the difference that it was not the individual banks that had to keep money in reserve. Rather, the central bank held the cash reserves of all the banks, allowing it to use that money to aid any banks in distress, thus making it possible for any single bank to safely survive a potential 'bank run'.

Modification of the discount rate at which the central bank lent fresh money to commercial banks. By lowering the discount rate, the central bank could provide an incentive for commercial banks to borrow new money.

---

67 In reality, the multiplying factor was slightly inferior because some transactions were conducted in cash.

Once this fresh money had entered the credit system, its impact would be amplified by the money multiplier mechanism, generating an increase in the money supply.

Open market operations. The third and final measure available to central banks to alter the size of the money supply involved the trading of government bonds. By either purchasing or selling bonds, the central bank could inject or withdraw money, respectively, from the economy. While the previous two measures were only employed sporadically, open market operations occurred continuously. Their primary function was to adjust for any unexpected effects of the use of the previous two measures 'in real time', in order to maintain the economy in a state of constant, but moderate, inflation. Moderate inflation, together with low interest rates, constituted a stimulus for the economy. Conversely, excessive inflation represented a risk factor for economic stability. The reasons for the latter are evident, and illustrated by numerous historical examples, from Germany's Weimar Republic between the two world wars to Chavez and Maduro's Venezuela in the second decade of the 21st century.

The growth trap

Up to this point, we have seen the 'positive' role that monetary expansion plays in growth economies, as well as the measures that governments could employ to generate and control it. However, monetary expansion had unintended consequences that ended up drastically destabilizing the late capitalist system, giving rise to new problems that – reinforcing those we examined earlier – contributed to its ultimate collapse. The third and final question will address these consequences.

What negative consequences did the monetary policy measures have on the late capitalist economies and societies, and why do we refer to these consequences today as a 'growth trap'?

The most direct negative consequence of monetary expansion had to do with the way it distorted the distribution of wealth. Contrary to what one might expect, after each injection of fresh money into the economy, inflation did not follow instantaneously. Rather there was a delay, the length of which corresponded to the time needed for companies to adjust their price lists to reflect the new size of the money supply. During those few weeks or months, the people who first gained access to the fresh money had the opportunity to use it *before* prices increased, to their obvious economic advantage. Among the first recipients of the fresh money were, in addition to banks and other financial institutions, their privileged customers with access to the best credit opportunities. These opportunities were typically only afforded to those who were most likely to repay them, thus excluding less affluent individuals. While small entrepreneurs could somehow manage to protect themselves from inflation by adjusting their price lists – something that, we must note, entailed substantial costs in terms of money and labor – salaried workers had to wait even longer before they saw their wages rise to compensate for the higher prices. Lastly, the unemployed saw their purchasing power reduced without any possibility of compensation. Although it was never described as such, inflation was thus a regressive tax in disguise, the cost of which weighed most heavily on the poorest segments of the population; a tax made even more insidious by the fact that the vast majority of the population were oblivious to its existence.

A second negative consequence of systematic and constant monetary expansion was closely linked with its apparently positive effects, detailed in the previous section. We have seen that inflation, in conjunction with the loosening of credit produced by the monetary injections, favored consumption over saving. The result was that at the turn of the century, the level of savings progressively fell to the point where many people started to fuel their consumption with debt.[68] The progressive weakening of the middle class only contributed to the acceleration of this process. Thus, while the share of global wealth allocated to salaries waned and the share that filled the coffers of corporations and financial institutions swelled, debt granted an increasingly impoverished population the purchasing power necessary to sustain their level of consumption and provide fuel for further purposeless growth.

To make matters worse, the problems generated by the swelling of private debt came against a backdrop of massive government debt.

---

68 A typical case is the United States in the early 21st century, where average savings were negative. See for example Guidolin, M., La Jeunesse, A. *The decline in the U.S. personal saving rate: is it real and is it a puzzle?* Federal Reserve Bank of St. Louis Review, 6:89, 2007, pp. 491-514.

These public debts developed due to a complex interplay of historical and political factors, of which a full examination is beyond the scope of this essay. As such, we will only briefly touch upon the most important elements:

- The tendency of states, in the decades following the Second World War, to use debt to fill the shortfall of public revenues with respect to public spending. These measures were taken in the (largely vain) hope that the growth stimulated by an increase in government spending would generate the additional revenues needed to pay back the debts incurred;
- The tendency of governments, especially those of representative democracies, to pursue expansive spending policies which could generate short term economic benefits, with immediate electoral advantages for those responsible. These policies were more often than not implemented at the cost of an increase in public debt, the long-term negative consequences of which were poorly understood by the electorate, and could hence be easily blamed on political rivals;
- The already discussed race to the bottom among states vying to attract foreign investment, which severely dented tax revenues.

At the turn of the millennium, the public debt of many countries had reached or surpassed their respective national GDPs and, combined with private debt levels, in some cases exceeded GDP by up to 300%.[69] The result was an increased vulnerability of both families and states when faced with recession, which ironically further bolstered the arguments in favor of perpetual economic growth. If growth stopped, however briefly, the impact on consumption, investment and employment would have been swift and severe, precisely because the safety net of savings was no longer there to soften the blow. The simultaneous crises that afflicted national welfare systems only served to aggravate an already tragic situation.

Hence, during the decades before the decoupling between economic growth and employment had fully manifested itself, monetary expansion appeared to be the ideal solution once again. More money in the economy meant more growth, more jobs and consequently higher

---

69 Gallino, L. *Finanzcapitalismo*, Einaudi, 2011.

fiscal revenues for states, which would have in turn allowed governments to reduce the public debt, or at least hold it steady. On the contrary, recession would have left governments with no choice but to increase taxation (thus worsening the recession), cut public spending (thus reducing people's well-being), or borrow more money (thus increasing the public debt further). In other words, the late capitalist societies were trapped in a vicious circle of escalating debt that could only be sustained with continuous economic growth, making a policy of monetary expansion seem unavoidable.

However, monetary expansion had a third distorting effect on the economic system, one that was perhaps even more dangerous than the first two. While banks and financial institutions could already reap huge profits by lending and investing sums of money that vastly outweighed the deposits in their vaults (through the mechanism of the money multiplier), lax international regulation of the financial sector led to the creation of novel and highly sophisticated speculative instruments, which exponentially multiplied their leverage. Fueled by the liquidity afforded by the continuous flow of fresh money into the economy, the financial sector bloated disproportionately, progressively dissociating itself from the material economy, upon which it nonetheless ended up exerting a growing influence.

From the range of constantly proliferating speculative instruments was born the practice of securitization. This essentially consisted of packaging the debts from loans (most of which were based on money that did not physically exist) and reselling them as bonds, which could then be freely traded or reinvested in the market. These bonds, generated in ever-increasing quantities, soon became the equivalent of a new form of money (or, technically speaking, quasi-money). As such, they represented *ipso facto* a further expansion of the money supply, drastically complicating any assessment or control of the money flowing through the economic system by states and central banks.

Adding to an already complex situation, a second new type of money became widespread at the end of the 20th century: the derivative. In its original form, a derivative was an agreement between two parties that bound them to exchange a certain quantity of goods at an arranged price, either within a specific time interval or at a definite point in time. However, over the years derivatives became subject to a series of modifications that inflated their speculative functions, while simultaneously severing their links to the material economy. These changes in the nature and use of derivatives resulted in their exponential proliferation, which converted them into a critical source of systemic instability. To gain some idea of their weight in the economy, in the year 2008 the total value of the global derivative market was already 21.4 times higher than that of the entire world's GDP, which then amounted to about $60 trillion – an increase of 600% compared to only a decade before.[70]

With its unrestrained growth and the reckless behavior of its main players, the financial sector wasn't just accumulating wealth independent of the material economy – it was doing so to the detriment of the latter. At the beginning of the 21st century, the immense market for derivatives, securitized assets, stocks[71] and debentures was managed according to logic and practices that totally ignored the economic and social value of the goods and companies that were being speculatively traded. Whether it was wheat or nuclear reactors, it mattered not to those who bet on derivatives. Similarly, the nature of the various goods and services produced by publicly traded companies made no difference to those who bought or sold their stocks. All that mattered were the profit margins, which were largely determined by the mere willingness of speculators to buy or sell the financial assets they controlled. In this way, financial speculation altered market prices independent of the mechanisms of supply and demand, distorting economic indicators and making it difficult for entrepreneurs to plan their investments. It also complicated the work of states and central banks, who saw their ability to anticipate approaching economic trends and prevent the ever bigger and more frequent speculative bubbles progressively weakened. Nonetheless, states and central banks were expected to address the havoc wreaked on society when those bubbles burst, providing aid to a financial and credit sector that combined growing economic – and therefore political – power with a lack of responsibility for the consequences of its actions. The onus ultimately fell on the backs of states, leading to further increases in public debts, which were now entirely out of proportion to the dimensions of the national economies, and therefore impossible to repay through the traditional route of taxation.

---

70 Serfati, C. *The current financial meltdown: a crisis of finance capital-driven globalization*, University of London, 2009. However, it must be noted that the figures quoted in the text refer to the nominal value of derivatives, while their real value was equal to the difference between the original market price that served as a reference for the initial bet and the price at the expiration date of the derivative. At the time of expiration, the parties would simply pay each other that difference, normally equal to only a fraction of the nominal value of the derivative.

71 It is estimated that, at the beginning of the 2010s, about 80% of the $120 trillion worth of stocks exchanged annually on the global stock markets were traded for purely speculative goals. Source: Gallino, 2011.

This was the historical context of the previously discussed progressive disconnection between economic growth and employment.[72] While their positive effects on employment became increasingly marginal, decades of expansive monetary policies aimed at incentivizing growth had led to a progressive financialization of the economy and soaring levels of debt, destabilizing the system and making those same monetary policies appear unavoidable. Meanwhile, in the background another crisis posed an even greater danger than the labor and debt crises, and demanded an urgent political solution. It is this crisis, more than any other, which illuminates the profound paradoxes of the late capitalist society that we have described up to this point.

On the brink of ecological disaster

While mainstream economists and politicians struggled to find ways to keep stoking the growth they deemed essential, a growing number of scientists and scholars were warning the world about the environmental consequences of not only a further expansion of the material economy, but even simply conserving production and consumption at their current levels. These warnings were not just theoretical: empirical data demonstrated that the late capitalist economic model was no longer sustainable from an ecological standpoint. What follows here is an overview of the situation at the beginning of the 21st century.

Earth's total surface area amounts to roughly 51 billion hectares. Of this area, around a quarter corresponds to the space where humans can survive and thrive, the rest being covered by deserts and oceans. This limited living space was the source of most of the renewable resources available on the planet;[73] if we divide it by the 7 billion individuals who inhabited the planet at the beginning of the century, we find that a sustainable ecological footprint corresponded to around 1.7 hectares per capita. However, by 2012 the average global consumption of resources had already reached 2.8 hectares per capita.[74] The gap, which amounted to 1.1 hectares, was filled by the exploitation of the reserves

---

72 Such disconnection, as we saw earlier, was to a good extent a consequence of the profound effects of technological innovation on workers' productivity.

73 Fisheries constitute an obvious partial exception.

74 *National Footprint Accounts 2016*, Global Footprint Network, 2016.

accumulated by ecosystems over the millennia. Moreover, these already worrying figures concealed deep distributive inequalities: in the same year, the per capita land-use of Indians was around 1.16 hectares, while for US residents it was a whopping 8.22 hectares.[75]

In this sense, the example of fresh water – among the most precious of resources to sustain human life – is particularly illuminating. Despite scientists raising the alarm about the progressive depletion of fresh water due to excessive use, the average American continued to utilize 575 liters per day, more than twice the 250 liters consumed by the average European and around thirty times the 19 liters consumed by an inhabitant of sub-Saharan Africa.[76] During the same period, between 20 and 30 hectares of forest were being cleared per minute, corresponding to an area the size of Greece every year, while it is estimated that between 50 and 200 species of plants and animals went extinct every day,[77] a rate hundreds of times greater than that estimated for pre-industrial times.

And if ecosystems, weakened by over-exploitation and over-burdened by waste, were slowing down the production of renewable resources, the stocks of non-renewable resources were also rapidly proceeding towards depletion. Aggravating an already dire situation, the inconsiderate consumption of resources, in addition to polluting the planet's air, water and soil, was generating a rise in global temperatures which threatened even worse ecological catastrophes.[78] Despite all this, states and international bodies continued to praise the energy-intensive lifestyles of the Global North, as if they were the greatest achievement of human civilization. Their infatuation was such that they actively promoted the extension of these lifestyles throughout the entire world,[79] something that would have required the resources of several planets to be remotely sustainable, even without taking into account demographic growth.

As usual, it was the science of economics that provided the

---

75 *Ibid.*

76 *Human Development Report 2006*, UNDP, 2006.

77 Wilson, E.O. *The diversity of life*, Penguin Press, 2001.

78 The apparent success in reducing greenhouse gas emissions that many European states boasted of resulted in actual fact from mere tricks of accounting. Emissions totals calculated only internal production, which in the context of deeply tertiarized economies was negligible. However, the excessive levels of consumption in Europe also represented a stimulus to foreign manufacturing, leading to greater emissions on a global scale. Of course, the British, French, Germans, Italians and Spanish were ultimately responsible for the greenhouse gas emissions and waste generated in the manufacture of the products they consumed, despite the fact that they were produced in other countries.

79 Actually, this was more or less the explicit objective of most international cooperation, and in particular of global bodies such as the World Bank and the International Monetary Fund.

theoretical legitimacy for this folly. The massive defensive expenditures needed to stave off the damages caused by growth were tallied as benefits in state accounting, as they contributed to the swelling of the sacred national GDP. After all, the diseases caused by pollution provided jobs to doctors and other medical staff, while the natural disasters exacerbated by climate change necessitated expensive public works, which in turn created employment and 'kept the economy going'.

The core argument used by the unrepentant apologists of perpetual growth arose in the 1970s, with the emergence of a new cult that accumulated millions of devotees over the following decades, and was ultimately adopted almost everywhere as a national religion. The cult went by the name of 'green economy', and the god it worshipped was known as 'sustainable growth'. Blinded by their own faith, the indefatigable clergy of the new cult repeated the mantra that technological innovation, by perpetually increasing the efficiency of production, would make it possible to reduce the energetic and material input needed for each unit of GDP *ad infinitum*. The sacred economic cake could then continue to grow in size, while simultaneously reducing the ingredients needed for the dough, and everyone would be able to indulge their gluttony in perpetuity.

Unfortunately, as with all faith-based cults, the dogma of the green economy did not reflect reality and failed to withstand deeper scrutiny. To understand why this was the case, a good starting point is the well-known equation $I = P \times A \times T$, proposed in the 1970s by Paul R. Ehrlich.[80] The equation calculates the aggregate impact on the environment of human activity (I) as a product of the population size (P), affluence (A; i.e. per capita consumption), and technological efficiency (T), the latter measured as the quantity of resources needed and the waste generated per unit of GDP. The fantasy upon which the creed of sustainable growth was based held that it would be possible to make per capita consumption (A) and the population size (P) grow continually, while at the same time reducing the aggregate environmental impact (I) through progressive and continual improvements in technological efficiency (T). Put another way, it posited a progressive decoupling between GDP and matter.

Here we must clarify a fundamental point about the nature of such a decoupling, which could assume two forms. A 'relative decoupling'

---

80 Huesemann, M.H. & Huesemann, J.A. *Technofix: why technology won't save us or the environment*, New Society Publishers, 2011.

defines a situation in which technological advancements reduce the resources consumed and waste generated per unit of GDP, while an 'absolute decoupling' defines a situation in which there is also a reduction of the quantity of resources used and waste generated at the level of the entire economy. Only when the latter is the case can one legitimately refer to growth as sustainable. In other words, if technological innovation allows for a 10% reduction in the resources needed for each slice of the economic cake but the economy as a whole grows by 20% in the same time span, the aggregate environmental impact rises regardless. Furthermore, if consumption continued to increase, as the advocates of the green economy insisted it must, and population growth could not be checked without impinging on personal freedom,[81] an absolute decoupling between GDP and matter would have been contingent on an accelerating technological efficiency that outpaced the growth of GDP.

In the real world, even though a *relative* decoupling did indeed occur throughout the 20th and 21st centuries, it was never even remotely sufficient to translate into an *absolute* decoupling. While nobody could deny that the cake required less and less custard and cream for each new slice, its size nonetheless rose so fast that in absolute terms an increasing supply of both was required. And if an absolute decoupling did not occur over the short term, it was implausible that it would occur over the long term, for two principal reasons.

The first reason concerns a phenomenon known as 'Jevon's paradox'.[82] This holds that in a free market system, there is a positive correlation between the efficiency of use of a particular resource and its aggregate consumption. This is because improved extractive or productive technologies translate into a greater supply of resources, lowering their market price, which in turn provides an incentive for the producers to use more of them. The result is a paradoxical acceleration of the depletion of natural resources: the abundance of the economy equates to the misery of the planet.

The second reason stems from the laws of physics themselves.

---

81 The growth trap went hand in hand with a similarly insidious demographic trap, which was not limited to the advanced economies. This demographic trap was created by the interaction between public pension schemes that were largely financed by the taxation of salaries, on the one hand, and a general lengthening of lifespan on the other. In this scenario, the sustainability of public spending depended on increasing, or at least keeping stable, the ratio between the working population and the elderly. As with the growth trap, it was the requirements of the late capitalist system (and more precisely its fiscal and redistributive sub-systems), rather than the needs of human beings, that constituted the main obstacle to resolving the pressing environmental challenges of the time.

82 Jevon's paradox is named after the 19th century economist who first observed the phenomenon in the use of coal by British industry.

Regardless of the pace at which technological innovation can boost productive efficiency, a strict material limit ensures that in the long term further gains in efficiency become increasingly difficult, and ultimately impossible. It is true that a car can be made with considerably fewer resources, perhaps by reducing the required energetic input, lightening the chassis and automating production and distribution. However, regardless of the sophistication of the technology used for its manufacture, a car – just like any other physical object – requires a minimum input of energy and resources to come into existence and fulfil its function. As technological innovation gradually shifts the efficiency of productive processes in the various sectors of the economy closer and closer to that impassable material boundary, the marginal reduction of the resources and waste needed for each additional unit of GDP approaches zero. Conversely, the growth of GDP follows an exponential curve. One hundred years of economic growth at a rate of 3.5% each year does not result in an expansion of 350%, but rather 3,100%. 3.5% annual growth represents growth with respect to the previous year, not to an arbitrary initial starting point. Thus two centuries of growth at 3.5% results in a GDP that is 972 times bigger, while after three centuries the economy is 30,000 times bigger, and so on. Even a mere 2% rate of growth – judged quite modest by the economists of the time – would in two thousand years result in an economy ballooning to 160 quadrillion times its initial dimensions. To be ecologically sustainable, such a rate of growth would require technological efficiency to improve by the same degree. This would mean producing footballs and teacups from single atoms, and ethereal cars fueled by the thoughts of their passengers (which unfortunately represent a considerable energetic expense in terms of calories!).

Such a fairy tale was the scenario yearned for by the prophets of sustainable growth. More than science and innovation, it would have required magic and fairy dust to make it a reality. As Herman Daly put it so long ago in the 1970s, the idea that it would be possible to decouple growth from material constraints by "angelising GNP is equivalent to overcoming physical limits to population growth by reducing the throughput intensity or metabolism of human beings. First pygmies, then Tom Thumbs, then big molecules, then pure spirits. Indeed, it would be necessary for us to become angels in order to subsist on angelised GNP".[83]

Armed with this realization, we can see that the proposal to substitute a growth driven by services for one driven by consumption is no more realistic a solution. The supply of services, be it legal advice or yoga instruction, also requires a minimum of energetic and material input. One illustrative example is the services involved with the packaging, distribution and promotion of fruits and vegetables, which in the time of late capitalism had a substantial impact on the total input of their production-consumption cycle.[84] Even the internet, with no apparent physical reality, was far from a zero-cost service in energetic terms. Considerable resources were required for it to function smoothly, many of which were dedicated to the production, distribution, maintenance and disposal of billions of computers, smartphones and tablets.

Similarly, the transition from a linear production-consumption cycle to a circular economy based on recycling was not a feasible solution. Linear and circular economic models are not mutually exclusive alternatives, but rather two points along a continuum, and the utopia of a fully circular economy is incompatible with the laws of physics, in particular with the second law of thermodynamics.[85] It follows that sustainable growth, which was never achieved in the short term, is by definition unattainable in the long term (if we exclude an extremely unlikely colonization of space). Rather, the only function of the sustainable growth dogma was to provide an excuse to politicians to procrastinate and further postpone an inevitable showdown between the economy and the ecosystems.

Human societies found themselves in a situation with no apparent way out, where politics and popular culture both encouraged the creation of economic debts to stimulate growth, the direct consequence of which was the further exploitation of the environment. For a graphical summary of the situation discussed up to this point, see Figure 4.

As the ecological reckoning drew ever closer, the more the economic cake grew in size, the more toxic it became. It was toxic for

---

83 Daly, H.E. *The steady state economy*, W.H. Freeman and Co. Ltd. Ed., 1972, p. 119.

84 Nemecek, T., et al. *Environmental impacts of food consumption and nutrition: where are we and what is next?*, in "International Journal of Life Cycle Assessment", 21 (2016), pp. 607-620.

85 The second law of thermodynamics holds that within an isolated system (such as, for all practical purposes, the Earth), entropy will increase over time. Every time energy is transformed by natural phenomena or human activity, part of it is dispersed and thus rendered unusable in the future. Although the process of transformation and dispersion of energy is constant and occurs even without human intervention, the latter inevitably accelerates it.

---

the environment, which grew saturated by waste and saw its reserves plundered. It was toxic for future generations, who were deprived of the resources essential for their well-being, squandered at a foolish pace by the late capitalist economy. It was toxic for those who managed to appropriate the biggest slices, which no longer provided them with any substantial benefit. Lastly, it was toxic for the majority of the global population, who were left with nothing but crumbs and condemned to a needless material and psychological misery.

Figure 4. The late capitalist economic model

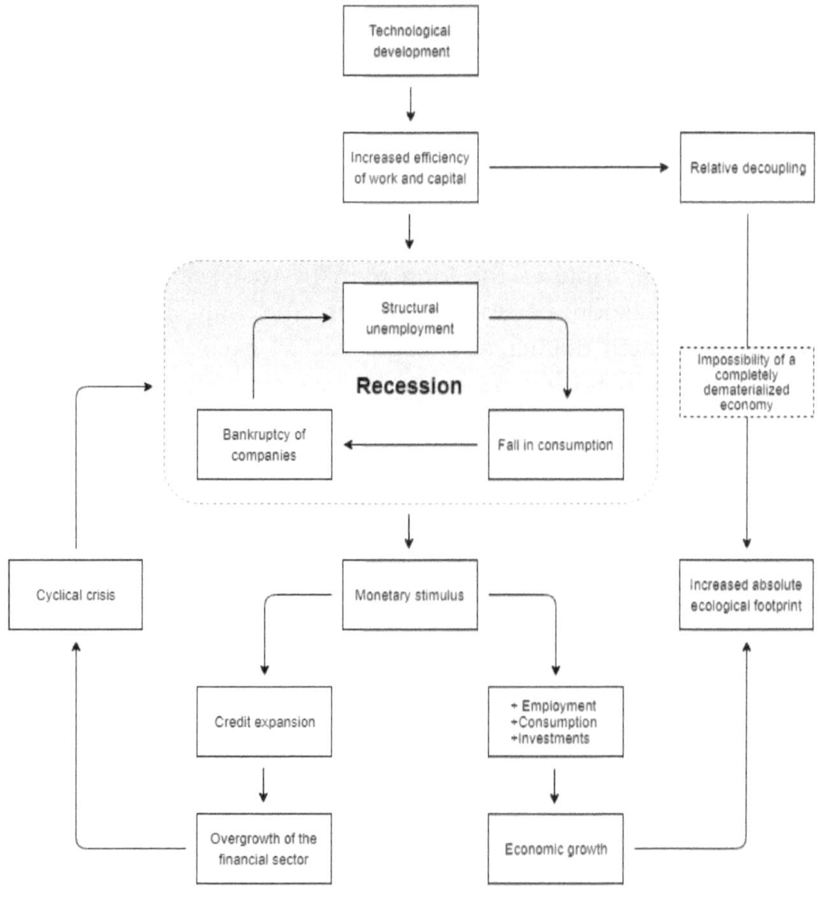

Politics between a rock and a hard place

At the beginning of the century, consumerism and productivism were still deeply rooted within the social fabric, despite the havoc they wreaked on the environment, the economy and on society. Whether consciously or not, most people continued to equate economic growth with the common good, consumption with well-being and career success with personal fulfilment. This blinded them to a simple yet disconcerting truth: if only people could free themselves from superfluous consumption, the production and supply of essential goods and services would have been possible with just a small fraction of the work that was mobilized in late capitalist societies. An equal redistribution of wealth, not contingent on work, could have then put an end to the nightmare of unemployment and transformed technological innovation from a source of problems into an opportunity for liberation. A reduction in superfluous consumption and emancipation from the chains of obligate work would in turn have increased well-being, while also substantially reducing the economy's impact on the environment.

Although the dominant economic discourse implied the existence of a trade-off between prosperity and the protection of ecosystems, this was not the case. The most intense pressures on the environment were largely a consequence of the foolish cycle of over-work, over-production and over-consumption. This cycle did not contribute to human well-being, and only served to pointlessly perpetuate the late capitalist system. The true choice was actually an easy one to make. It was the choice between the unsustainable and ephemeral unhappiness that was condemning the world to ecological collapse, and the sustainable well-being that could save it.

As we saw earlier, the twin ethics of work and consumption were diffused among the population through an extensive institutional network that included the education system, mainstream media and social services, and was further consolidated and perpetuated by social imitation. This network saw problems where there were potential solutions (less work, consumption and growth) and saw solutions in damaging problems (superfluous consumption, pointless work and monetary expansion). The result was the creation of a collective filter between perception and reality that stymied any attempts at change. Unsurprisingly, a pervasive and widespread cognitive dissonance thus simmered in the population when the noxious effects of growth began to threaten the common good, when over-consumption began to damage personal well-being, and when work turned into a ridiculous circus of unnecessary activity. Put simply, the world stopped making sense. Old certainties crumbled away.

Reality, no longer hidden away under the epistemological rug weaved by economists, finally emerged into the realm of politics. However, politics had no means of understanding this reality, at least initially. As a result, the first reactions were schizophrenic and clumsy attempts at combining conflicting opposites: incentives to grow while reducing environmental footprints, the promotion of consumption while struggling against waste, investment in technological innovation while clinging to job-centered policies. Predictably, far from remedying society's ills, these efforts ended up aggravating them. In the first few decades of the new millennium, politics found itself between a rock and a hard place. On the one hand, rising public and private debts, systemic unemployment and wealth inequalities made the pursuit of growth seem unavoidable. On the other, a deepening environmental crisis demanded that growth slow down as soon as possible.

Any proposal to cease economic growth and redistribute the immense wealth generated by productive technologies clashed with the myopic interests of the economy's major players (multinational corporations, big financial conglomerates etc.), contradicted the work ethic that all political parties of the time placed at the core of their platforms, and was even opposed by those victimized by the status quo – especially the poor and middle class – who ironically would have only stood to gain from such structural changes.

The economic filter between perception and reality was sufficiently pervasive and powerful to persuade the unemployed to feel ashamed of their situation, and to beg their governments for a ride on the rusting carousel of superfluous work, instead of fighting for their rights.

To complicate the situation further, the population at large was unaware of the structural causes of the environmental and labor crises, and clamored for solutions that were wholly inappropriate for the problems at hand. In the over-developed countries, in which the absence of tangible advantages generated by growth made change most urgent, the prevalence of media-centered democracies made the process of reform even harder.[86] The rapid succession of electoral

---

86 Reeves, A. *Mediacracy: rise and decline of a political model*, self-published, 2086.

cycles favored the implementation of short-term policy solutions, whose immediately visible effects allowed their proponents to reap rewards at the ballot boxes. Conversely, the long-term negative consequences that these myopic 'solutions' often entailed could be easily ignored, because they would extend well beyond the term of any single government and could therefore be readily blamed on political opponents. Moreover, the sensationalist media circus which surrounded politics smothered the possibility of genuine public debate, such that the *communicability* of an idea, rather than its *quality*, was the main factor determining its electoral success. Thus simple ideas and catchy slogans dominated talk shows and electoral debates, at the expense of nuanced ideas and well-reasoned arguments.

This 'stage democracy' did not favor intelligent leaders, but rather propelled charismatic figures to power, whose proposals were focused on marginal issues that the electorate could immediately grasp. Hence, precisely when far-reaching reforms were desperately needed, parliaments and presidential palaces were filled with men and women with short sight and booming voices. To soothe the discontent of a profoundly disoriented populace, these leaders went so far as to propose a revival of a past that was in equal parts beautiful and fictional: the United States needed to be *great again*, Europe needed to defend its white and Christian roots, and all were exhorted to shun the immigrants, driven from their lands by poverty, arriving to seek a better future. With a surprising spark of political ingenuity, it was these immigrants, unable to vote, who were paradoxically converted into the ideal scapegoats on whom to vent the anger and insecurity of a desperate electorate. With poorly concealed pleasure, the populist leaders of the wealthy North proclaimed them responsible for the decline of the welfare state, for the labor crisis, for the soaring public debts, and even for the periodic waves of imaginary criminality which so delighted the mainstream media of the time.

Still, while politics, imprisoned by the structural and cultural cage of late capitalism, looked in vain to the past for a key to free itself, the seeds of the future, long hidden in the depths of the social fabric, began to germinate. And it would not be long before the sprouts they unleashed would push into the cracks at the base of the cage, weakening its foundations and triggering its inevitable collapse.

SILENT REVOLUTIONS

In just three centuries, from the end of the 17th to the beginning of the 21st, the world's population transitioned from poverty to abundance. In the same period, most human labor shifted away from the production of staple goods and towards the production of increasingly inessential goods and services. While in the agricultural societies of the 17th century the great majority of workers were occupied producing food, in the industrial societies of the early 20th, jobs were already concentrated in the manufacturing sector. Only fifty years later, the tertiarization of the economy and the automation of material production led developed countries to specialize in the creation and supply of services, from healthcare and travel agencies to logistics and finance.

Despite its ups and downs, the growth of the economy until then had proceeded hand in hand with an improvement in human well-being. Yet well-being, unlike GDP, does not obey the principle of maximization, and beyond certain thresholds of consumption and production it stops increasing and slowly starts to diminish. Ignoring this reality, the late capitalist societies, instead of easing up on the accelerator of growth, pushed the pedal to the metal with renewed energy.

It eventually became common knowledge that only three people out of every ten needed to work in order to abundantly provide for everyone. Technology had replaced arms and brains as the primary engine of global production. Even so, rather than rejoicing and laying the groundwork for a post-work society, there was widespread talk of decline and a renewed push for creating novel and increasingly pointless jobs through over-consumption, planned obsolescence and the ceaseless creation of gadgets and entertainment. As is now known, the effort was useless, as although technological unemployment appeared to be fading in the 1980s, it returned with a vengeance in the first decades of the 21st century. Meanwhile, superfluous jobs, over-production and over-consumption were not simply failing to generate further well-being: they were endangering the ecosystems that constituted its very foundation. Hence, the specter of looming environmental disaster, the labor 'crisis' and the toxic societal effects of the culture of excess ended up shedding light on the intrinsic limits of the late capitalist model.

And then, when all seemed lost, something changed. As has happened many times throughout human history, a tiny spark was lit, which in a few short years ignited a fire that burned the old world away. Some, in retrospect, called it a revolution. However, if a revolution it was, it was one with neither weapons nor bloodshed. It was also a revolution largely devoid of revolutionaries: just ordinary people that little by little awakened from a long sleep. Left behind scattered on the bed were the now useless and absurd visions of an already forgotten dream – the consumed well-being, the duty of work, the redemption of growth. With open eyes, none of it made sense anymore.

Who produced that first spark? Who sowed the first seed? It may have been the unemployed, when for the first time they organized to claim a share of the immense wealth generated by the machines. It may have been the youth, when they responded to the impoverishment of their lives by shunning old idols and abandoning their temples. Perhaps more realistically, it may have been the systemic crisis of late capitalism, without which neither of these would have found the strength to act. To this day it remains unclear, and in truth it matters little. As in the first part of the book, I will concentrate here on the overarching structure of the changes, leaving the specific historical events in the background.[87]

If we hang up our historian's garb and don that of the sociologist, we discover there were three of what we might call the seeds of change.[88] The first involved the redistribution of wealth, welfare systems and the labor market; the second pertained to the education system; the third concerned the reigning political order. Each of the next three chapters allows the story of one seed to unfurl, in this order.

The sprouts that emerged from those three seeds found mutual support and strength, and wound up building the foundations of a new world. Without those three seeds, the fall of the late capitalist system would almost certainly have resulted in unprecedented social, economic and political decline. Without those three seeds, the prosperity that we enjoy today might never have seen the light of day.

---

87 Although the second part of the book concentrates on the situation in Europe, it still reflects the core changes that occurred in parallel in other parts of the world (with slight variations, due to different socioeconomic and institutional contexts).

88 For clarity of exposition, for the time being we will set aside the cultural dynamics which made these changes possible (and were in turn reinforced by them). A general discussion of this topic can be found in Chapter 7.

3 WORK AS A CHOICE

At the dawn of the new millennium, the cultural climate was slowly changing, particularly in Europe. Post-consumerist and post-laborist movements and communities (from Degrowth and the Transition Towns to the Downshifting and Tiny-House movements) saw their followings grow among the population. As a result, the lifestyles of many people, especially the young, begun to change.

The cognitive filters placed over reality by the twin ethics of work and consumption began to falter, and political proposals that were dismissed as utopian just a few years earlier started to be seriously considered. Some were discarded, while others were implemented for a short while and then withdrawn. One, however, proved to be extremely effective, and remains to this day. By itself, it constitutes arguably the core component of the solution to the occupational, economic, social and environmental crises initiated by the late capitalist system.

On account of its profound institutional and historical impact, the philosopher and historian Angélie Perrin recently defined it as "the greatest socio-political innovation since the time of Athenian democracy".[89] It was the pan-European Universal Basic Income (UBI).

Universal basic income, welfare and the role of the state

"Frustra fit per plura quod fieri potest per pauciora".[90] it is pointless to do with more what can be done with less. This maxim, formulated by 14th century friar William of Ockham, was long ignored in the field of social engineering. In the era of late capitalism, the suggestion that a simple idea could prove more effective than a complex web of norms, institutions and laws was totally alien to the mind-set of those charged with administering the state. Above all, this was because their own usefulness and the salaries which depended on it were directly proportional to the complexity of the bureaucratic apparatus which

---

89 Perrin, A. *A political history of Europe*, Acropolis, 2078, p. 37.

90 William of Ockham, *Summa Totius Logicae*, I. 12, 1323.

---

they navigated. That a simple idea could solve problems that had vexed humanity since the dawn of history – from absolute poverty and petty criminality to corruption and worker exploitation – must have appeared to them as the feverish delusions of fools. Nonetheless, this was exactly what happened when the UBI was first introduced throughout Europe around half a century ago.[91] Its implementation is exceptionally simple, almost banal: every man and woman of age receives a monthly income from the state, an identical sum for each individual. This sum is sufficient to satisfy their basic needs, in terms of housing, food, personal hygiene and so on. No conditions are attached to receiving this income, and no solicitation is necessary. It is granted to the rich and poor, young and old, employed and unemployed alike.

Given that its very nature was radically incompatible with the dominant laborist and meritocratic ethics, we should not be surprised that these reforms were initially met with fierce opposition from traditional political factions. The Right alleged that the scheme would be economically unsustainable, subsidize the lazy and inevitably lead to a more powerful and centralized state; the Left decried that the payments did not favor the economically and socially disadvantaged. As such, it came as a shock to many when the introduction of the UBI brought about quite the opposite: limiting state interference in the economy, decreasing public spending, improving market efficiency and reducing economic and social inequalities. The inability of the established political factions to foresee this outcome can be traced back not merely to widespread and ill-concealed cultural prejudice, but also to the mistaken belief that the new reforms would add to, rather than largely replace, the old mechanisms of selective welfare[92] provisioning.

As we mentioned in Chapter 1, between this century and the last the meritocratic imperative dictated a careful selection and screening of potential recipients of public services and subsidies. Unemployed people who actively sought a job on the market had more rights than those who did not; immigrants from favored countries received preferential treatment; women, the elderly, young people and large families were all allocated specific aid, and so on. Such a complex

---

91 Although a universal basic income scheme was not truly implemented until well into the 21st century, the idea has a much longer history. It had been proposed in various forms throughout the ages by many well-known intellectuals of various ideologies and backgrounds, from Thomas Paine to John Maynard Keynes, and Bertrand Russell to Milton Friedman.

92 By 'selective welfare' I refer to the network of public services, subsidies and benefits whose supply and access by individuals was contingent on their satisfaction of specific requirements, be they economic, social or other. Examples would be unemployment benefits and aid aimed specifically at society's poorest.

system of selection demanded enormous human and financial resources to manage it. It also demanded the existence of a vast apparatus of control to screen for those eligible to receive public aid and combat fraud by those falsely claiming it. The result was that only a small percentage of the money allocated to public aid actually ended up in the pockets of its intended beneficiaries.

The UBI solved this problem once and for all, raising this proportion to almost 100%. It did so by replacing most of the old, selective welfare services, and rendering obsolete the gargantuan bureaucratic apparatus that administered them. With the disappearance of the entitled, the cheaters also disappeared, along with the need to combat them. Public spending could thus be reduced, and became more efficient. The following list offers a small selection of the many welfare services that were made obsolete by the introduction of a UBI:

- *Unemployment benefits.* These were public benefits granted to individuals in a situation of involuntary unemployment. Their substitution with a UBI allowed governments to dismantle the labyrinthine and expensive bureaucratic apparatus that had mostly existed to select and control those entitled to aid. However, there was another, more important result of the abolition of unemployment benefits. Because they were conditional upon unemployment, these benefits actually represented an economic disincentive to work. The strength of that disincentive was proportional to the difference between the salary that new employment would bring and the quantity of the benefits. As such, this disincentive was most apparent for those who, for various reasons (such as a lack of qualifications), could only access undesirable and low-paid jobs. It was not uncommon for these people to prefer to work cash-in-hand rather than looking for work on the open market, in order to avoid losing their access to benefits. This phenomenon, known as the 'poverty trap', is today a distant memory; the UBI, unlike unemployment benefits, does not constitute a disincentive to work, for the simple reason that taking a job does not entail its loss.

- *Minimum wage.* This was a measure by which the state

imposed a minimum monthly remuneration for employed workers. In addition to the considerable expense of guaranteeing it was correctly applied, the minimum wage, far from eliminating the exploitation of workers, simply moved it off the books, where wage conditions were often far worse. By abolishing the need for people to work to satisfy their basic needs, the UBI has today made it much more difficult for companies to find desperate workers to exploit. All of this was achieved without requiring any regulation from the state.

- *Social services and aid aimed at the poor and homeless.* One of the most important effects of introducing the UBI was the definitive elimination of absolute poverty. Since the UBI is sufficient to meet the basic needs of all individuals, the poor simply disappeared, rendering these social services obsolete.

- *Public pensions.* With the waning role of human labor in powering the economy, public pensions were no longer a suitable solution for supporting the elderly. Today, the UBI guarantees a decent life into old age for everyone, with no exceptions, leaving those who still desire to subscribe to private pension schemes free to do so. Unlike the mechanisms of selective welfare, the institution of public pensions was dismantled gradually, to avoid the justified objections of the taxpayers who had already paid for their pensions. These people initially received a supplement, on top of the UBI, to compensate for the shortfall with respect to the payments that would have derived from their curtailed pension schemes.

The streamlining of the welfare system allowed for a significant reduction in the staff required for its administration at all levels – local, national and continental. Its advocates had previously justified the substantial cost of the welfare state by the idea that public employment constituted a useful, though expensive, relief valve for unemployment. And yes, the system of selective welfare did indeed require an enormous number of workers; this, however, was not because of its utility, but rather due to its remarkable inefficiency as a mechanism for redistributing wealth! Once this inefficiency was eliminated by the introduction of the UBI, these workers became superfluous. However, they were not abandoned to their destiny: the money once misdirected to paying their salaries would contribute to funding the UBI. Just like everyone else in society, these former civil servants, despite losing their jobs, could use the new unconditional economic support to reinvent their lives, both professionally and personally. This fact contributed, among other factors, to weakening the resistance to the job cuts among the population.

The advantages of dismantling the old system of wealth redistribution, however, were not only economic. Among its many positive effects were the elimination of the paternalism and stigma associated with the previous welfare model.[93] People were finally freed from the humiliation of having to beg the government for help, and from being obliged to adhere to the stringent conditions that came with it. More often than not, the false empowerment of the ancient 'activation policies' in practice translated into forceful and often mortifying paths of reintegration into the labor market and social environment. On the contrary, the UBI grants people the trust and respect required to develop their own life project, in a socioeconomic system that does not highlight their shortcomings or impose a standardized model of what a 'good citizen' should be.

Compared to the selective welfare system that it replaced, the UBI scheme also offers the considerable advantage of having transparent and predictable costs. In fact, its total cost can be obtained by simply multiplying the number of adults in the population by the level of the UBI, making any attempt to defraud the public on the part of bureaucrats and politicians exceptionally difficult. In the context of this essay, this simple multiplication allows us to demonstrate that the implementation of a wide-scale UBI scheme was already possible, at least in developed countries, at the beginning of the 21st century.[94] As an example, let us take Italy in the year 2015 (although the result would be the same for the year 2010 or 2020). The adult population of the country at the time was around 50 million. The introduction of a UBI of 500 euros per month, sufficient to cover the basic needs of each individual, would have cost the state exactly 300 billion euros,

---

93 See Chapter 1, section '*Workfare and meritocracy*'.

94 OECD, *Basic income as a policy option: can it add up?* Report, May 2017.

according to the simple calculation reported above.[95] This amounted to less than the annual expense for public pensions alone, a total of 335 billion euros. Hence the implementation of a reform that was not only financially viable but also economically efficient and socially necessary was prevented, for many years to come, purely by the unfortunate alliance of the myth of meritocracy with the lingering legacy of the work ethic.

Before proceeding to analyze the main economic and social impacts of the introduction of the UBI, we must pause for a brief digression on the issue of migration. As is well known, a truly universal access to basic income, although ethically desirable, would have almost certainly driven an uncontrollable flow of migrants into the countries which implemented it. This motivated the initial decision to make UBI conditional on citizenship. In this sense, the fact that individuals had to reach adulthood (defined as over 18 years old in most countries) before receiving the UBI served to effectively prevent 'birth tourism'.[96]

Some social services remained active, charged with the task of meeting the needs of the immigrant population that did not yet have access to this new mode of wealth redistribution. With the spread of UBI schemes in more and more countries, these services could be progressively reduced, to concentrate only on the immigrants that hailed from countries where the UBI was not yet available.[97]

Currently, one of the main priorities of the United Nations is the extension of the UBI to all member states, with the long term goal of creating a global UBI scheme financed internationally through a common fund, a prospect that is hopefully not too distant.

Socioeconomic consequences of a revolutionary reform

When it was finally implemented, the UBI put an end to the odious late capitalist dichotomy between a system of production increasingly

---

95 We arrive at 300 billion euros by multiplying the adult population of 50 million by 500 euros per month by 12 months per year.

96 There are of course other reasons that compelled the implementation of such a threshold, among which is the fact that granting the UBI to children would likely have created incentives for a 'procreation business' that was better avoided, for obvious reasons.

97 Immigrants from countries with an active UBI scheme that does not cover them abroad are still ineligible, as they always have an opportunity of survival in case they decide to return to their home country.

independent of human labor and a system of wealth redistribution built around work.[98] It achieved this by transforming work performed on the market from an economic necessity into a personal choice. Today, for the first time in history, nobody is forced to work to survive, and the little human labor that is still needed for the optimal functioning of the economy (in terms of maximizing the well-being of the population) is allocated by the law of supply and demand to those who are most motivated to carry it out and most skilled in its execution.

Once material survival was removed from consideration, the line between professional and vocational activities became blurred. Today everyone is occupied with some kind of activity but, unlike in the past, these activities are a choice that reflect the passions and talents of each individual. Although there are still firefighters, scientists, traders and artisans, there are no longer *involuntary* firefighters, scientists, traders and artisans. The most undesirable, tiring and tedious jobs have not disappeared, but automation has substantially reduced their number. Furthermore, by virtue of a free labor market with no more wage slaves to exploit, they are now among the most profitable. These days a waste collector can easily earn more than a scientist.

The increase in the intrinsic motivation of the remaining work force manifested in a significant growth in productivity which, combined with the deregulation of the job market and the streamlining of public bureaucracy, translated into an increased efficiency of the economy as a whole.

As the UBI serves as a safety net for the unemployed, it had the effect of producing a more elastic labor supply.[99] This in turn increased the bargaining power of workers, albeit by a moderate amount. In this way, every time technological innovation further reduces the overall need for human labor in the economy and correspondingly shrinks salaries, the number of workers willing to work on the market also diminishes, restoring the balance between demand and supply and at least partially compensating for the fall in wages (see Figure 5).

In the long term, however, additional measures would be required to avoid the emergence of a society dominated by a small number of rich and super-rich who controlled the technological capital, amid a

---

98 See Chapter 2.

99 In political economics, the labour supply measures the inclination of individuals to sell their time and work in exchange for a salary. All other factors being stable, if the labour supply is elastic in relation to salaries, a decrease or increase in wages produces, respectively, a decrease or an increase in the number of individuals willing to work.

population that existed barely above the poverty line thanks to low salaries and a modest UBI. For this reason, whenever the labor supply is significantly in excess of demand, the level of the UBI is increased.

Figure 5. Dynamic equilibrium of salaries in the presence of a guaranteed universal basic income (1)

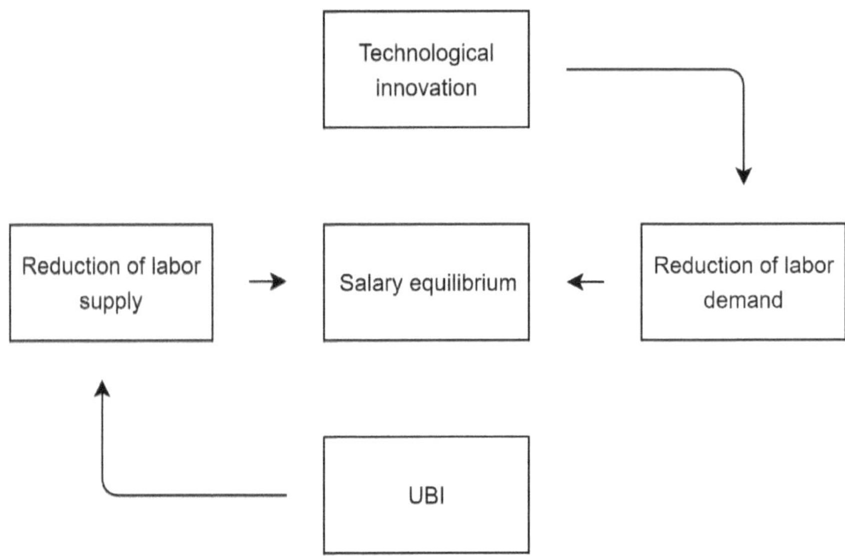

This provides an incentive for more people to leave the labor market,[100] counterbalancing the decline in salaries and redistributing the growing profits generated by technological capital among the population at large (see Figure 6).

Of course, if the old fiscal systems centered around taxation of wages had remained unchanged, state revenues would have progressively declined along with employment, putting the financial sustainability of the UBI scheme in jeopardy. As such, a progressive shift in the focus of taxation from salaried work to capital was inevitable, if only because it was the latter which had assumed a central role in the economy. More specifically, taxation was increased on

---

100 It is important to stress that many of these people continue to work in the market, but do so in an autonomous way. As we will see in Chapter 7, self-employment is standard in today's marketplace.

material and technological assets, financial transactions and inherited wealth.[101] At the international level, enormous progress was made in evening out the differences between states in terms of rates of capital taxation. Together with stricter regulations on the international movement of capital, this finally put an end to the race to the bottom among states that had for decades enriched the super wealthy and multinational corporations at the expense of the masses.

Figure 6. Dynamic equilibrium of salaries in the presence of a guaranteed universal basic income (2)

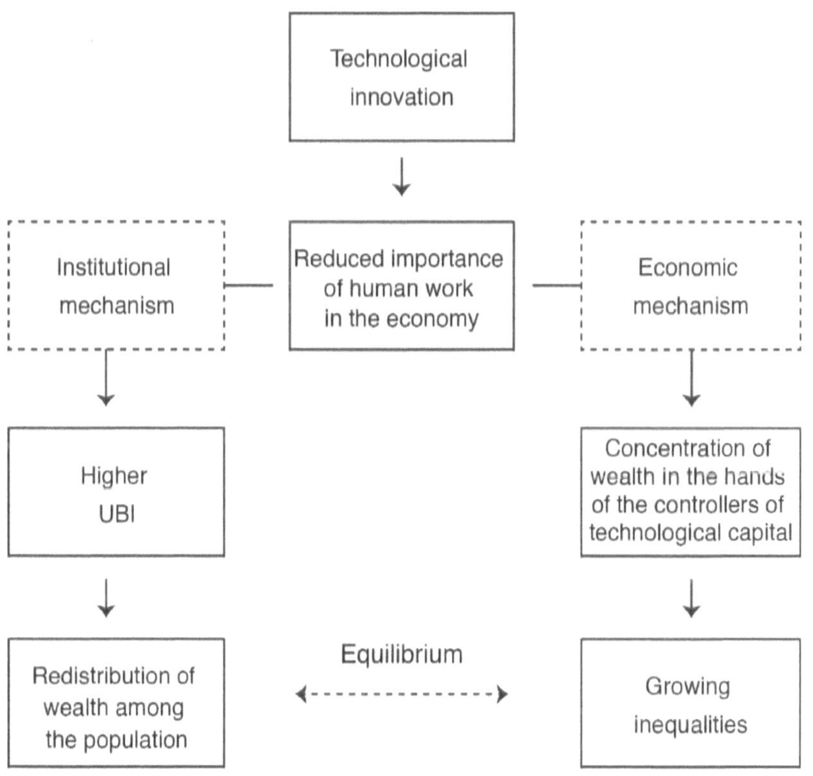

However, the UBI not only revolutionized the workings of the economic system and the allocation of public services. The decoupling

---

of personal survival from employment reduced the imbalance of bargaining power between companies and workers, leading to a substantial improvement in working conditions. At the same time, the elimination of absolute poverty produced a considerable reduction in petty crime, especially property crimes such as shoplifting, burglary and pickpocketing, historically associated with conditions of social and economic deprivation. For the various mafias – both legal and illegal – it became more and more difficult to recruit youngsters who were willing to do anything for money. The result was a decrease in spending on policing and the judiciary, which in turn freed up yet more public resources. Each of these factors also contributed to easing social conflict and stress levels in the population, with a consequent amelioration of mental health problems and a reduction in the public spending required for healthcare.

The UBI replaced the stigmatizing paternalism of the late capitalist welfare state with the opportunity for all to fully develop their ideas and talents, an opportunity that in the past had been the exclusive privilege of the sons and daughters of the wealthiest families. The chance to pause and consider, without being forced to sell oneself to survive, allowed many brilliant men and women to work on long term projects. The number of scientists, musicians, artisans, philosophers, jugglers, writers and monks increased; the number of PR agents, marketing experts, door-to-door salesmen and bureaucrats decreased. Self-employment and small businesses flourished. Useless jobs, in terms of aggregate well-being, disappeared, and useful ones multiplied. Freed from the chains of labor, human beings chose to specialize in what the machines cannot provide: art, culture, science and knowledge.

Addressing the criticisms of the neo-laborist movements

The fear that the UBI would have left most people leading a lazy life that alternated between the couch and the fridge, born of an economistic view of human activity, turned out to be unfounded.[102] As

---

102 In reality, the empirical evidence that this would not be the case was overwhelming even before the large-scale introduction of universal basic income. Since the 1970s, numerous experiments with UBI had been conducted at the local and regional level in such diverse sociocultural and economic contexts as the United States, Canada, Namibia, Kenya, the Netherlands and Mongolia (among others). Almost without

history itself makes evident, human beings possess an innate drive towards activity and personal development. At the dawn of capitalism, the dominant economic discourse channeled this drive towards the accumulation of money and material property, pitting man against man. Even though this had served a key purpose in a world characterized by material scarcity and an abundance of work, it had become completely dysfunctional within late capitalist societies in which an unprecedented material abundance was coupled with high levels of structural unemployment.

As we all know, the awareness and acceptance of the need for a systemic change did not come easily. Decades of relentless indoctrination in the laborist ethic had convinced our ancestors that the effort demanded and the salary awarded were the best criteria on which to judge any human activity. According to this logic, the more stressful or well-paid a person's job was, the more useful and worthy of respect it must have been. Likewise, any human activity that was performed voluntarily out of joy and for free was by definition of little use (if only because it did not contribute to the growth of the sacred GDP!).

The structural crisis of late capitalism opened people's eyes, leading to a spreading awareness that reality was indeed different from how the orthodox economics textbooks described it. A large part of the work with which people flagellated themselves was not only pointless, but also damaging to the environment and the well-being of those who performed it. Confronted with this historical fact, the current criticisms of the UBI by the neo-laborist movements, based on the apparently unacceptable presence of a few 'loafers' who use it to indulge in passive and lazy lifestyles, lose all meaning. First, one must recognize that their number is much lower than the number of superfluous workers who thronged the late capitalist economies at the turn of the millennium. Second, while the daily chores of many of those superfluous workers were essentially performed under coercion, for today's 'loafers' their inactivity represents a conscious lifestyle choice. When we take into account that the contributions of the superfluous workers to societal well-being was negligible anyway, we can appreciate that at least today's loafers live in serenity. Put another way, the UBI exchanged a

---

exception, the result was not soaring dependence and passivity but rather an increase in independence and enterprising spirit. In fact, the observation that even those who could afford not to work – principally wealthy people – generally continued to do so, provided ample basis to reject the idea that, in late capitalist times, the primary incentive to work was the threat of hunger.

melancholy and coerced uselessness, comprised of tens of hours a week spent in an office, shop or factory, for a happy and voluntary uselessness. What's more, the loafers, lacking the internal motivation to be active, would also be particularly inefficient workers. In other words, even if we accept the flawed logic of laborism and productivism, in economic terms the loss of the contribution of today's loafers would be much more negligible than one might think.

Placing a non-existent problem at the core of their arguments, the neo-laborist movements advocate for the pan-European UBI scheme to be abolished and replaced by a legally-enforced redistribution of work among the population. This would be achieved by introducing legislation to limit working hours to a strict maximum. Despite the force with which its proponents press for it, it is an old idea that appears utterly inadequate once the costs and social consequences of its implementation are taken into consideration.

First of all, unlike the UBI scheme, it would require the creation of an expensive apparatus of control to effectively prevent people from working more than their legal quota, for instance by taking a second job or working extra hours cash-in-hand. Incidentally, this is exactly what happened in all of the economies that implemented similar measures during the first decades of the century, to the point where the average hours worked regularly exceeded the legal limit. A second flaw of the neo-laborist proposal concerns its inability to address poverty. With the UBI eliminated, the reintroduction of selective economic aid and social services, with all their myriad costs and inefficiencies, would necessarily follow to compensate for its loss. Thirdly, the proposal values neither personal freedom nor market efficiency. A forced redistribution of work would infringe upon the liberty of both those who want to work more and those who do not wish to work at all, which would diminish the average motivation of the workforce and reduce its productivity.

We could continue with a rather long list of reasons for which the neo-laborist proposal of work sharing is inferior to the UBI, but the most important of all concerns that linchpin of the modern economy, technological innovation. As we move into the 22nd century with most global production generated by technological capital, the absence of a redistributive system independent of wages would render it impossible to avoid a progressive concentration of wealth into the hands of the owners of that capital. Imposing ever-higher minimum wages to attempt to offset that concentration would only have the effect of providing further incentives to accelerate the automation of the economy and fuel black-market labor. The widespread poverty that would result would eventually make the reimplementation of the UBI unavoidable.

For all of these reasons, the idea of mandatory work sharing represents at best a temporary solution to problems which have already been solved, and at worst a sort of sadistic time machine programmed to drag us all back to an undesirable past.

4 A SCHOOL OF FREEDOM

The crisis of consumerist and laborist ethical values on the one hand, and the introduction of Universal Basic Income on the other, set in motion a profound reconfiguration of society. In the previous chapter we touched upon some aspects of this reconfiguration, which we will describe in further detail in chapters 6 and 7. In this chapter we will instead focus on its effects on the education system.[103]

As work progressively lost the central role it had once occupied in the economy and in people's lives, the old, standardized, hierarchical model of mass education was deprived of all purpose, and was eventually retired. In its place, a new way of learning emerged: voluntary, democratic, tailored to the individual and less rigidly structured.

A student-centered learning

We might succinctly express the most salient difference between the new and old models of education by saying that the new paradigm does not revolve around teaching. Teaching, in this sense, is defined as a didactic method whereby one person transmits knowledge to another. In modern schools nothing is really taught, but much is learnt, with knowledge proceeding directly from the curiosity of each student. Rather than a passive object to be filled with instructions and lectures, the student is an active subject in a process of learning that unfolds as a journey of discovery, of the world and of the self. Each student's journey is by necessity different, and cannot follow pre-established paths or yield to external goals. Each goal is personal, each journey is individual. The role of the school is merely to provide the assistance, tools and resources to make each student's journey possible, without erecting barriers to their exploration or leading them down pre-established paths. Of course, this does not mean that there are no signs to guide the way or destinations to reach, but simply that each student

---

103 One could be forgiven for thinking that education constitutes a secondary factor in the context of the great changes that human societies underwent over the course of the 21st century. Nevertheless, it is important to keep in mind that schools constituted the training grounds in which entire generations were inculcated with the rules and rites of the late capitalist world, and in which they learnt to accept them as natural.

chooses these for themselves.

What does this mean in practice? First of all, it means the total absence of standardized curricula. With the exception of a mandatory preliminary phase which is required to acquire fundamental skills such as reading, writing and arithmetic, the final decision on what to study, when to study it and in what order is left entirely to the individual student. To each and every student an adviser is assigned, whose task is to help them develop a personalized study plan, which can be revised and revisited along the way, based on their specific interests, aspirations and talents. One student may opt to study zoology and literature, while another chooses contemporary history and drama. Of course, some disciplines are not immediately accessible due to their complexity. When eight-year-old Luca tells his adviser he is interested in astronomy, he will be told about the difficulties inherent in its study. If Luca chooses to persist in his goal of learning astronomy, his adviser will help him to develop a personalized learning plan with the aim of first cultivating the knowledge of mathematics and physics that are a prerequisite for the study of astronomy. Weeks or months may pass before Luca begins to actually approach his chosen discipline, but the fact that this arduous journey moves him towards his personal goal, rather than an externally imposed objective, ensures that he commits himself to it with a passion.

The abandonment of standardized curricula rendered the ancient subdivision of education into academic years and terms obsolete. For the same reason, the segregation of class groups according to age yielded to a more efficient subdivision according to disciplines of study. In modern schools, there are classrooms dedicated to the most diverse disciplines: from history to biology, psychology to literature, modern languages to geology. Within them, students of various ages study together, each following their own tailored program.

This personalization of curricula went hand in hand with a profound reconfiguration of the way knowledge is acquired: from being imparted to a group by an authority figure, to being an individual and self-directed endeavor. Each student enjoys the autonomy to explore the vast array of written and audio-visual materials at their disposal – mostly in digital form, through the numerous computers available to use in each classroom –, following the educational path designed in conjunction with his or her adviser.[104]

---

104 Traditional lectures have not disappeared. Today they are freely available to every student in digital form, through constantly updated

---

The autonomy afforded to each student does not exclude the possibility of group activities and seminars, as we shall see, but it does make every success a personal triumph, nourishing the pupils' confidence in themselves and their own abilities. It also allows everyone to tailor their learning strategy to their personality, which improves the quality of learning. However, the fact that learning has become an individual endeavor does not mean that young people are abandoned and left to fend for themselves. In every classroom there are always a number of learning mentors present, each specialized in the classroom´s associated study area, ready and waiting to help whoever may be struggling with their personal study. Unlike the teachers of traditional schools, the intervention of the learning mentor is never imposed, and always comes in response to an explicit request for assistance by the student.

The dissolution of the authoritarianism that characterized the old system of education is also reflected in the role currently played by exams. In the past, the purpose of exams was to evaluate the students rather than to help them understand and learn from their mistakes. Put another way, their function was more social and economic than didactic: they served to define rankings of 'merit', which would then regulate access to further education and careers in both the public and private sectors. Today, students still undergo testing, but with a different purpose. There are two types of test. The first provides certifications which attest to the student's theoretical and practical knowledge, while the second are self-evaluation tests that are used by students and advisers to track their progress towards the mutually agreed objectives in the personalized study plans. Generally speaking, the first type spans broader areas of knowledge, while the self-evaluations tend to be narrower in focus. The topic and timing of the tests are agreed upon jointly by the student and their adviser, and the test papers are then prepared and corrected externally by experts in the field, to guarantee impartiality. Unlike tests in traditional schools, the correction of the papers involves no judgement, and no marks are assigned. Each student is simply informed about what mistakes were made in the test, and is provided with indications on how to address these shortcomings. At this point, the student reviews what he failed to understand before proceeding with further studies. In this way, learning advances smoothly and no-one is forced to waste their time studying

online archives.

topics that are too advanced for their level of knowledge, as was often the case in the traditional education model. For exams linked to a certification, the student is also informed whether or not they passed the test. Under no circumstances are pupils punished for a bad result.

Before we proceed, it is worth pausing to consider what has been perhaps the most controversial aspect of the modern educational system: that students learn voluntarily. Although parents are obliged by law to send their children to school, once there they can decide not to study and do something else instead. For example, they can choose to relax in the school playground, or play football with their friends. However, most children *decide* to study. This would come as quite a surprise to our ancestors, and it is easy to understand why. For most of modern history since the emergence of the first nation-states, compulsory education had been the rule, whether it was foisted upon students by their family or by law. That said, it becomes much less surprising once what is now a rather banal truth becomes clear: regardless of the educational system in place, learning always implies an active effort by the student, without exception. This effort can spring from the innate curiosity of human beings, which children and adolescents possess in abundance, or it can derive from an external imposition, whether formal (mandatory attendance) or in the guise of a system of incentives and punishments (good and bad marks, praise and blame). However, these two forms of motivation do not produce the same result. As demonstrated by two centuries of psychological and pedagogical research, the human mind is stimulated to greater exertion by things it has chosen rather than things forced upon it, and more by interest than by discipline. To opt for obligation over self-determination is to transform the student from a subject into an object of education, from a *creator* of meanings and ideas to a *creature* to be tamed for a goal which he cannot legitimately contest. In the case of the late capitalist education system, the only tangible result of that decision was to force entire generations of students to spend ten or more years sitting behind a school desk. Some of them learnt, but most simply attended. On the contrary, to exalt self-determination over obligation means to identify the student as a subject and thus unleash his creative energy and innate curiosity.

As the success of democratic and libertarian schools had already made clear in the 20th century, young people, when free to choose, *want* to learn.[105] Today, the vast majority of students spend fewer hours sitting at a school desk than their forebears did but learn much more, because their learning results from a conscious choice rather than from an imposition.

Autonomy responsibility and democracy

In today's schools, the freedom of each student arises within well-defined norms of coexistence, at the core of which is the fundamental principle that each person's freedom finishes where the freedom of others begins. In practice, this means that the students' decision-making autonomy entails responsibility for the choices that they make.[106] Autonomy and responsibility cannot exist separately without soon starting to deteriorate. Autonomy without responsibility rapidly declines into licentiousness. Meanwhile, responsibility without autonomy is reduced to mere obedience. This was the case for late capitalist students, whose only choice was between subjugation and rebellion, conformity and deviance. There was no space for dialogue because everything – from the school curricula to lesson timetables – was mandated from above. It follows that the 'good student' of the early 21st century was 'responsible' for her education in the same way that a loyal subject of an absolute monarchy is responsible for the political events of the kingdom.

In modern schools, autonomy and responsibility are genuine, because they are bound together by common rules that create the space for individuals to choose their own paths. Choosing not to study is a legitimate decision, which triggers no punishment or formal sanction, but those who make this choice effectively renounce their opportunity to develop their knowledge and talents. This is a different situation to that of a student who decides to violate the common rules, for example by failing to attend a seminar he had registered for without informing the school in advance of the reasons for his absence. In this case, the student would face a sanction depending on the circumstances and type of infraction, normally some kind of activity that contributes to the public interest, whether that of the school or the local community. The sanction is fair, because it is rooted in a responsible choice taken freely by the student. If he had initially decided not to attend the

---

105 A pioneer in this sense was Summerhill School in England, which had already proposed and implemented a libertarian and democratic education by 1921.

106 Sella, F. *Autonomy and responsibility of students in contemporary education*, Carmeli, 2096.

seminar and thus had not registered, he would not have triggered the sanction. Having opted to do so, he assumed responsibility for his own attendance. This system has a strong educational value in itself: it teaches young people to think for themselves, make decisions and accept the consequences these decisions entail.

Table 1. A comparison between two education models

	Late-capitalist education	Modern education
Curricula	Standardized and rigid	Personalized and flexible
Attendance	Mandatory, activities to a great extent pre-determined	Mandatory, free choice of activities
Learning style	Collective and externally imposed	Individualized and self-directed
Relationship between students and school staff	Vertical and hierarchical. Modelled on factories and boot camps. Imbalance of power between students and teachers	Horizontal and democratic. Students' autonomy subject to respecting common rules
Tests and exams	Aimed at establishing public rankings (socioeconomic function). Centered around marks	Aimed at identifying learning problems (educational function). No marks are awarded

If freedom (defined as the opportunity to be and develop in agreement with one's own nature) is the beating heart of modern education, democracy is doubtless its rational mind. Although the spirit of democracy and participation runs through the entire spectrum of interpersonal relations within the modern school, its core is undoubtedly the school parliament. At regular intervals, the parliament holds sessions in which many things are decided, from the use of bicycles in the playground to the proposal of a new seminar or workshop. Students, advisers and learning mentors are all welcome to participate. Throughout the week before each meeting, anyone can suggest a proposal through the school's online platform, or lend their support to the proposals of others. Those that raise the most interest are then discussed in the parliament, which eventually decides to accept or reject the proposal based on a vote. All the participants in the parliamentary session, from the nine-year-old students to the fifty-year-old advisers, have the right to vote. As the majority, this effectively puts students in a strong position relative to the adults, which is at least partially compensated by the more developed rhetoric and persuasive skills of the school staff. Participation in meetings is not mandatory, and often only a minority will participate. However, any decisions taken are binding for everyone.[107] While the freedom to decide instils the values of responsibility and self-determination in young people, their experience in the school parliament gives them the chance to learn the principles of dialogue and democracy.

Almost half a century after the reform of the education system in Europe – which today is quickly spreading to the five continents – its effects are reflected in the daily actions of every adult. The submissive workers and passive voters mass-produced by the old educational system gave way to active and creative citizens, who see work and study as sources of joy, and political participation as an integral part of their everyday lives.

As we will see in the next chapter, the new system consolidated and stabilized the changes set in motion by the UBI and the widespread diffusion of post-laborist and post-consumerist values, paving the way to a new manner of seeing and living politics in everyday life. However, before moving on to examine this aspect, it is worth stepping back for a moment from our theoretical analysis to take a closer look at a student's typical day in a modern European school.

---

107 Of course, some aspects of school life remain beyond the power of the school parliament. Specifically, the fundamental norms of the school and the libertarian and democratic principles at its core are immune to modification.

A typical day in a modern European school

Milan, April 2097. It is 9 o'clock. Just like every morning, Laura enters her school, a multi-level building with a large garden on the ground floor.

Taking advantage of her time spent commuting by metro, Laura has already reviewed her schedule for today, agreed upon with her adviser Marco: a workshop on community gardening at 9 AM, two hours of individual study in the classroom dedicated to historical and geographical studies, and in the afternoon a seminar-debate on the causes of the decline of English as the global lingua franca. While thinking about the seminar in the metro, Laura can't help smiling to herself – she had proposed the topic at the previous session of the school parliament, and against all odds her proposal was met with great enthusiasm and immediately approved by a large majority.

When Laura steps into the school's greenhouse, the workshop is just about to begin. Eric, 20, is the volunteer chosen by the parliament as its coordinator. He invites all the participants, a total of eleven students of ages 8 to 15, to pick up their gardening tools and take a seat. As is often the case, the workshop is practical and theoretical in equal measure, in line with what experts refer to as 'experiential learning'.[108] Laura immediately notices the presence of her friend Abdul, who is two years older than her. As far as she knew, his main interests lay in informatics and engineering – she never would have expected to see him at a meeting about community gardens! When asked, Abdul explains that he has been working on a new online platform on the topic and, following his adviser's suggestion, he thought gathering some first-hand information on the topic wouldn't hurt.

It is now 10:30. The workshop has just finished and, judging by the participants' pleased faces, it was a success. Upon leaving the greenhouse, Laura logs into the school app on her *POMUD* (Portable Multimedia Device) to sign in for the next session, which is scheduled for a few days later. She still has more than three hours until the seminar-debate begins at 2 PM. Her original plan was to continue her study program on the political system in China during the Han dynasty, but she is too excited about the afternoon debate, so she decides to go

---

108 Moretti, E. *Experiential learning. A toolkit for young researchers and explorers,* self-published, 2095.

to the language classroom to gather her thoughts in preparation for the meeting. On her way there, she stops at the school canteen to have an orange juice. Meanwhile, she informs her adviser of her decision via *POMUD*.

While taking the stairs up to the language classroom on the third floor, Laura remembers what her late great-grandfather had told her years ago about school when he was a student in the 2030s. In those days, he said, there were still teachers, and the standard teacher-centered lessons involved groups of 20 or more students – not only for practical disciplines like acting and horticulture, but also for subjects such as math and philosophy! The worst part, however, was that the students could neither decide what to study nor when to study it. Nor were those decisions taken by someone who knew them well, but rather by some ageing bureaucrat in a dusty office in the capital, who most likely knew nothing about the interests and passions of the individual students. Thus the bureaucrat painted everything with a broad brush and established a curriculum that was identical for all. Her great-grandfather had added that this could not have been any other way; given the collective nature of education in his time, personalized curricula were utterly unimaginable.

When she arrives at the language classroom, Laura takes a seat at one of the available desks and turns the computer on. In the classroom there are students of all ages: some reading, some watching video-lectures, some partaking in online language exchanges with students of other European countries, and some doing exercises or interactive activities. Among the 15 students present, Laura notices her friend Sara, who at 11 years old is a foreign language enthusiast. At that moment, Sara is raising her hand to ask Chris for help. Chris is one of two learning mentors in the classroom and specializes in French and Esperanto. Sara appears to have some problems understanding the meaning of a paragraph in the French grammar book she is studying. Chris helps to clear her doubts, and Sara thanks him. Before going on to help another student with his hand raised, Chris reminds Sara that there are still some places available for the French conversation workshop scheduled for this afternoon, in case she is interested in joining.

One hour later, Laura has gathered all the information she needed and feels ready for the seminar-debate. However, there are still two hours before it begins, and it isn't lunchtime yet. Laura checks her *POMUD* and sees that Marco, her adviser, is currently available. She decides to take the opportunity to contact him and requests an immediate appointment. Marco accepts, and Laura goes to his office on the 4th floor. The two discuss Laura's upcoming exams, agreed at a previous meeting, and Laura informs him that she wants to postpone her exam on the political history of the Han dynasty by one week in order to have more time to prepare. Marco makes a note of this.

Returning to the ground floor garden, Laura meets three friends that have decided to take advantage of the beautiful spring morning to relax and play outdoors. They had asked Laura to join, but she declined due to her busy schedule that day.

After having lunch together with her friends, Laura goes to the classroom chosen for the afternoon's seminar-debate, one of many that the school makes available for the collective activities approved by the parliament. Giulia, one of the learning mentors and the moderator of today's seminar, welcomes Laura and invites her to take a seat. Following a brief presentation on the current state of academic research on the topic, Giulia declares the debate officially open. Thirty-four students of various ages participate.

After almost two hours of lively discussion in which Laura is one of the most active participants, it is time to go home.

5 FACELESS DEMOCRACY

A democracy can survive without an informed and politically active population, but it cannot function as it should. In Europe as elsewhere, the dominant rhetoric in politics and the media for more than a century had emphasized the sanctity of the 'will of the masses', brushing aside the importance of a responsible and conscious voting choice. The result was political regimes at the mercy of an uninformed and passive majority, which regularly fell prey to populist leaders of various persuasions. Incidentally, this problem had little to do with the level of education of the citizenry. Having a degree in engineering or medicine did not confer the ability to make better voting choices than someone with only basic high school qualifications. What would have made a difference was exactly what was lacking most in the late capitalist era: an electorate that had the time and the will to carefully examine political issues and critically analyze the proposals of the candidates.

Even so, it would not be fair to accuse our ancestors of intellectual laziness and lay the entirety of the blame for this state of affairs at their door. The real underlying factors at the heart of the issue were complex, as described in the first part of the book, and by their nature transcended any single individual. The first factor concerned the strong social, cultural and economic pressures on citizens that led them to devote the vast majority of their time and energy to career and consumption, leaving little room for politics. The second factor had to do with a widespread utilitarian conception of life that, although undoubtedly functional to the perpetual growth of GDP, was barely compatible with an individual search for the common good. People worked for personal success, or at best for the well-being of their families; they relieved their tensions and sought quick thrills through consumption. Neither purpose was served, at least directly, by being properly informed and participating in the political life of their communities, and thus such pursuits were judged by most as being unworthy of attention. Finally, the third factor consisted of a political and electoral system dominated by the media, which promoted instantaneous and superficial messages that, although effective in provoking an immediate emotional response from voters, were ill-suited to informing them about the real substance of political proposals.

The Universal Basic Income and educational reforms, in harmony with the spread of post-consumerist and post-laborist values in the wake of the crisis of the late capitalist model, went a long way towards addressing the first two factors. Finally protected by a safety net against poverty, people began to shift their priorities away from the economic sphere and towards the political. They became engaged in informing themselves and demanded more opportunities to participate in the political process. This change was led by the youngest generations, whose education had endowed them with both the ability to think critically and an active and non-utilitarian relationship to knowledge. The result was the emergence of a social and political environment which was favorable to the search for a solution to the third and final factor. Most modern historians see that solution in the rise of a new democratic regime that soon became known as 'faceless democracy'.

According to its most famous definition, a faceless democracy is characterized by "the central role given to information and political debate and for a high degree of depersonalization of representation".[109] The use of the adjective 'faceless' stresses the rupture with respect to the 'stage democracies' that preceded it, in which electoral success and political consensus was predicated on the exploitation of mass media communication and the stage presence of politicians and party leaders. Originally emerging in Europe in the 2050s, the faceless democracy is rapidly becoming the standard model in a growing number of countries around the world. In this chapter we will examine its main features.

A politics of reason

If the way politics proceeded in the old representative democracies was akin to product marketing, then the way modern faceless democracies function is closer to the competition between rival scholars. Researchers present evidence and elaborate hypotheses, in the form of journal papers or other types of academic publication, in order to deconstruct the theories of others or to bolster their own, thus winning the support of an informed public (the scholarly community). Conversely, marketing is a process by which competing firms develop seductive messages that aim to engineer a preference for their brand

---

109 Long, S. *Faceless democracy. A new model for Europe*, Exen Press, 2061.

among a generally uninformed public (the consumers) by tapping into their emotional and psychological biases. In the academic marketplace of ideas, content tends to prevail over form, whereas in marketing form prevails over content. What's more, the effort expended in the development of a successful marketing strategy does not enhance the quality of the products that it peddles, whereas the process of conceiving better forms of argumentation enriches the internal coherence, and thus the quality, of statements and theories. In this sense, the competition among scholars is more cost-efficient than the competition among marketed goods, and ensures that the public ultimately receives a better result.

In the old representative democracies, politics functioned according to the logic of marketing. The presentation of a party's proposals hinged on slogans and charismatic leaders, with the goal of eliciting strong emotional reactions from a public (the citizens) that was largely ignorant both of how political and economic institutions really worked, and of the content of the party manifestos. The consequence of this was the rise to power of politically short-sighted leaders with a powerful stage presence. On the contrary, in modern faceless democracies, politics works according to the logic of academic competition. During the election campaign, the parties present their proposals exclusively in written form, making them freely available to all voters through public institutional platforms (both online and offline) that are shared by all parties. Political rallies and electoral propaganda are prohibited. The different proposals are then discussed by nonpartisan journalists, who analyze each and provide comment on their implications and the strength of their arguments. The media are required to dedicate an equal amount of time to covering each proposal.

The depersonalization of election campaigns has had many positive effects on the overall quality of both political proposals and the candidates who forward them. First of all, the written word, unlike speech, transmits its meaning in a relatively aseptic environment, depriving the slogans and rhetorical sleight of hand of most of their emotional impact. Secondly, the prohibition of public speeches on behalf of the candidates shifts the focus of voters away from their appearance, body language and voice and towards the substance of the manifestos that they represent.[110]

---

110 Incidentally, the depersonalization of politics considerably reduced the cost of political campaigns. Today, each party gains and loses votes

While political rallies and electoral propaganda are forbidden, public debates are commonplace. The main difference with respect to the past is that debates take place exclusively online, and asynchronously. There is an interval, typically a few hours, between the arguments of each candidate to allow the other participants to carefully consider them and craft complex and thoughtful responses. In this way, the televised debates of old, dominated by personal accusations, sarcasm and slogans, gave way to profound discussions on the substance of political proposals, where high quality academic research is often cited in support of key statements and declarations.

The new system has also led to a democratization of access to political power, which in the past was preferentially conferred on individuals with great charisma, highly developed rhetoric skills and hypnotic body language – all talents undoubtedly useful during a political rally, but tragically useless when it came to making wise political choices. While the essential personality trait for electoral success in the era of late capitalism was charisma, today it is the ability to reason. Replacing politicians who were good at speaking with politicians who are 'good at thinking' constitutes perhaps the greatest accomplishment of the new democratic regime, marking "the transition from a politics of feelings to a politics of reason".[111]

Active participation and the informed voter

The progressive emancipation of individuals from the economic and cultural pressures that coerced them to over-work, together with the simultaneous decline of consumerism, opened up new opportunities for people to engage in self-expression and sociality. For the first time in history, citizens now have both the economic stability and the time required to become informed and consciously participate in a common political project.

Because of this, during the last half century the degree of political participation in Europe has grown in terms of the proportion of citizens involved, but above all in terms of the overall level and quality of their engagement. New approaches to deliberative democracy (many

on account of its arguments and projects, rather than due to the charisma of its leaders and support, or lack of it, from lobbyists.

111 Foglia, A. *Towards a politics of reason*, Plans Trivium Press, 2069, p. 27.

of which involved public consultation) were devised and added to the traditional mechanisms of representative democracy. This afforded citizens and politicians ample opportunities to meet, both face-to-face and through purpose-built online platforms, in order to discuss and debate the critical policy decisions and jointly craft potential solutions. Before long, citizens were involved in not only choosing between political projects but also shaping them, particularly at the local level. Of course, there was an expansion of direct democracy, with the extension of referendums to cover most issues of normal administration.

In a similar manner to what happened to students following the implementation of educational reforms, the greater opportunities for participation afforded to citizens went along with greater responsibilities. Now that the once-ubiquitous obligation to work has decayed away, there are no excuses left for ignorance. The validity of each vote is subject to meeting a minimum threshold of knowledge about the competing proposals and the functioning of the relevant economic and political institutions.

The current focus of political campaigning and debates on the content of policy proposals would be in vain if the vast majority of voters had continued to base their electoral preferences on emotion and instinct. In order to avoid this, all citizens that choose to vote in elections or referendums are required to submit two questionnaires along with their vote. Like the vote itself, these forms respect the anonymity of the voter. One is composed of general questions about the characteristics and functions of the electoral system, parliament and various governing institutions. The other probes the voter's familiarity with the content of the manifestos of all the parties in the elections – not only those he wishes to vote for – or, in the case of a referendum, about the core arguments for and against the proposal that is subject to a vote.

The drafting of these questionnaires is entrusted to an independent technical commission and must be subsequently ratified by parliament. Questions are designed to be easily understood and are thus posed in plain language, avoiding the use of a technical or unusual vocabulary. The level of difficulty is pitched so that a person of average intelligence and education would only need to read each manifesto once or twice to be confident of answering the vast majority of the questions correctly.[112]

---

112 A custom algorithm randomly selects questions from a pool of thousands of possible variations, in order to prevent their memorisation by

These forms are scrutinized so that *only* the votes of citizens who have correctly answered at least 80% of both questionnaires are considered to be valid.

<u>**Table 2. Core differences between faceless democracies and traditional representative democracies**</u>

	Traditional representative democracies	Faceless democracies
Political campaigns	Focus on form. Centered around slogans and personal accusations	Focus on substance. Centered on manifestos and rational debate
Voting style	Uninformed, emotional vote	Informed, well-considered vote
Political candidates	Charismatic	Intelligent

Naturally, as in the past there are still people who by nature are uninterested in politics, and decide for various reasons not to inform themselves, despite having access to all the economic support and time they would need to do so. In order to meet the needs of this segment of the population, in some countries a system of micro-proxies was introduced. Thanks to this system, any single citizen is free to delegate his vote to another, who is authorized to cast their ballot on their behalf. To prevent the rise of a system of vote trading and political favors, the proxies are governed by a set of strict restrictions:

- No more than one proxy per voter;

- The proxy system does not apply for local or regional elections;
- It is only possible to delegate votes to first or second degree relatives;
- The proxy must be renewed before every election via a certified form.

Faceless democracies promote a higher degree of accountability among political representatives. Citizens who are aware of the core points of every political proposal ensure that candidates think twice before making false promises, because once they assume office they know they will be judged according to their efforts to fulfil them. Today, everybody knows the main proposals of political candidates, but few remember their faces. In contrast, in late capitalist times only a small fraction of the voters were aware of the specific proposals of candidates, while their faces appeared everywhere in the streets and in the media. Thus, once they took power, politicians could generally discard their promises with little consequence in terms of their support. It is not surprising that those who were most disadvantaged by the new system were the populist leaders who had built decades of electoral success on slogans and voter ignorance. This shift in focus away from individuals in political campaigns and debates brought arguments and reasoning back to the center of the political arena. Meanwhile, the expansion of free time available to the average citizen and the introduction of minimum knowledge requirements for voting generated the informed public that is essential for the efficiency and proper functioning of the system. In this respect, it can be argued that faceless democracies paved the way for wiser and more effective political choices, whose longer-term consequences we will examine in the third and final part of this book.

TOWARDS A CIVILIZATION OF WELLNESS

Today we live in what has been defined by many as the most prosperous age in human history.[113] From a social standpoint, the so-called 'golden ages' of the past were anything but prosperous. The Renaissance was surely not prosperous for the vast mass of poor that thronged the beautiful cities of 15th century Europe. America of the early 20th century was certainly not prosperous for its exploited and poorly organized workers, accurately depicted by Howard Zinn in *A people's history of the United States*.[114] The comparison is even harsher with the late capitalist era, when prosperity was a privilege granted to a select few in the Global North, while its price was paid dearly by the entire global population, present and future. That price included the foolish over-exploitation of the planet's resources; the overload of ecosystems through an excessive production of waste; the exploitation of billions of poor souls whose only misstep was to be born in the wrong place at the wrong time; the millions of migrants rich in misery and poor in luck, turned away from the borders of opulence; the frantic and alienated lifestyles of corporate executives who, in order to gain access to the 'winner's circle', were willingly transformed into the gears that kept the system moving; and so on, demonstrating that the prosperity of late capitalism existed to a large extent only in the fervid imagination of mainstream economists. On the contrary, the prosperity of the present is not a privilege of the few but a right that is granted to a growing part of the world's population. Not only that: it is a prosperity that does not weigh on the shoulders of future generations, nor on the planet.

Chapter 6 is devoted to a description of the huge economic and institutional changes that, building upon the reforms described until now, made that prosperity possible. Chapter 7 focuses instead on the social and cultural aspects of that change, and gives a brief overview of life at the gates of the 22nd century.

---

113 Among others, see Morel, E. *The second short century*, Cassio, 2087; Matveev, V. *Elements for a post-capitalist sociology*, Merriam Publications, 2091; and Becker, F. *A brief history of human well-being*, Ocean Press, 2092.

114 Zinn, H. *A people's history of the United States*, Harper Perennial, 2005.

6 THE END OF GROWTH

When it became clear, around the turn of the millennium, that the unemployment generated by technological innovation was crystallizing into a structural feature of the late capitalist socioeconomic model, it put policy makers in a difficult position. The apparent choice was between an endless provision of monetary stimuli in order to generate growth, maintain consumption and keep employment to some degree stable, or to do nothing and bear passive witness to an economic recession and a contraction of fiscal revenues (with predictable effects in terms of electoral success).[115] Faced with what was to become known as the growth trap, politicians were forced to 'choose' the first option. However, the only result of this was to postpone the inevitable reckoning for a few more decades and exacerbate existing problems, above all that of a ballooning ecological impact that dwarfed the scale of terrestrial ecosystems.[116]

As we now know, the occupational, economic, financial and environmental crises became structural, gnawing at the very foundations of the consumerist, productivist and laborist values that upheld the late capitalist economic system. Much ink has been spilled on the chaos, protests and proposals that ensued. Finally, after decades of dithering, the convergence of soaring social tensions, structural unemployment and gaping wealth inequality forced Europe to act,[117] giving rise to the reforms described in the second part of the book. Largely unbeknownst even to their own proponents, these reforms would later provide policy makers with the means and strength to definitively dismantle the growth trap.

The growth trap dismantled

The first step towards dismantling the growth trap was to end the

---

economy's dependence on (more or less) full employment. As we saw in Chapter 2, this dependence was linked to the recessive cycle which, in the context of work-centered fiscal and redistributive systems, inevitably followed each sharp drop in employment (see Chapter 2, Figure 3).

Deprived of any income other than their salary, laid-off workers in the late capitalist era reduced their spending and lived off their savings. This dented private sector profits, with companies responding by cutting staff, thus generating further unemployment. Ultimately, spiraling unemployment would eat into public revenues, in turn leading governments to cut spending and rack up ever-higher public debt.

The solution to this problem was found in the reform of the redistributive and fiscal systems described in Chapter 3. A large part of the expensive welfare services of the early 21st century was replaced by a single pan-European Universal Basic Income scheme, which provided the economic system a means of wealth redistribution that was independent of work. Supported by the UBI, the unemployed could at least partially conserve their purchasing power, sustaining both private sector profits and savings and thus weakening the recessive cycle. Meanwhile, a thorough overhaul of fiscal systems shifted their focus from taxing salaries to taxing capital, boosting the long-term financial sustainability of the UBI scheme, while simultaneously severing the traditional link between public spending and employment levels.[118]

All this laid the groundwork for the second fundamental step of dismantling the growth trap: the easing of the electoral pressure on politicians to keep employment levels stable. Newly liberated from the cognitive filter that the work ethic had represented and now protected from poverty by the UBI, citizens' political preferences re-oriented towards post-laborist policies. The historically all-important policy objective of almost all governments to provide full employment withered away, paving the way for opportunities that only a few years earlier had seemed unthinkable. Among them, the most important was doubtless the establishment of a serious debate on the urgent need to transition from a growth economy to a steady-state economy, that is an economy whose stability does not depend on an endless increase of production and consumption. The arguments for such a transition,

---

118 The avoidance of capital flight owes almost exclusively to great efforts on the part of the international community to stipulate preliminary agreements that aimed to reform the fiscal systems of the planet's major economies in a coordinated way.

discussed in the first part of the book, were indisputable. However, the effective communication of these arguments to the electorate, convincing them to support this change at the ballot box, would not have been possible without the earlier transformation of European political regimes into full-fledged faceless democracies.[119]

In Europe of the 2050s, reason-based politics won out over emotion-based politics, finally bringing to power leaders who were prepared to begin a change that had been put off for far too long. At this point, only two obstacles remained to definitively dismantling the growth trap: the first was the instability caused by the bloated financial system, at the core of which was the institution of the fractional reserve; the second was the enormous public debt of most states.[120]

The first problem was easily solved with a proposal that had been put forward by ecological economists for decades. This was to raise the cash reserve ratio to 100%, forcing banks to keep all of the money available in their deposit accounts. As we saw in Chapter 2, the fractional reserve system was the principal culprit behind both growing public debts and the continuous financial bubbles that characterized late capitalist economies.

In order to avoid shocks to the financial system, the shift to a 100% cash reserve ratio occurred gradually, over the course of around 10 years. Banks, which had for years accrued much of their profits from interest on loans of fictitious money created by the money multiplier mechanism, started to act once again as simple financial intermediaries. Today, their profits derive mostly from keeping a commission on the interest obtained through lending money on behalf of their clients, as well as from providing financial services for a fee.

With the money multiplier mechanism eliminated from the credit system, the financial leverage wielded by large speculators was also significantly reduced. More specifically, the practice of securitization shrank considerably, and the trade in derivatives was prohibited outright. The lost link between savings, loans and investments was restored, and the speculative bubbles of old became no more than a sad chapter in the textbooks of economic history. The financial sector was reduced in size and regained a proper balance in proportion to the material economy.

The large public debts of nation states were by now the only

---

obstacle that prevented the achievement of a steady-state economy, in Europe and elsewhere. In this case the solution was also political, taking the form of a painful (yet fruitful) multi-year international mediation in view of a common goal. On the one side were the interests of institutional and private creditors, while on the other there was basic common sense – the protection of the planet and the well-being of future generations. Common sense ultimately prevailed, and the debts of most states were reduced and restructured. Humanity emerged more united from the numerous national and political divisions of the old world. With this final step, the growth trap was finally dismantled.

Figure 7. The growth trap dismantled

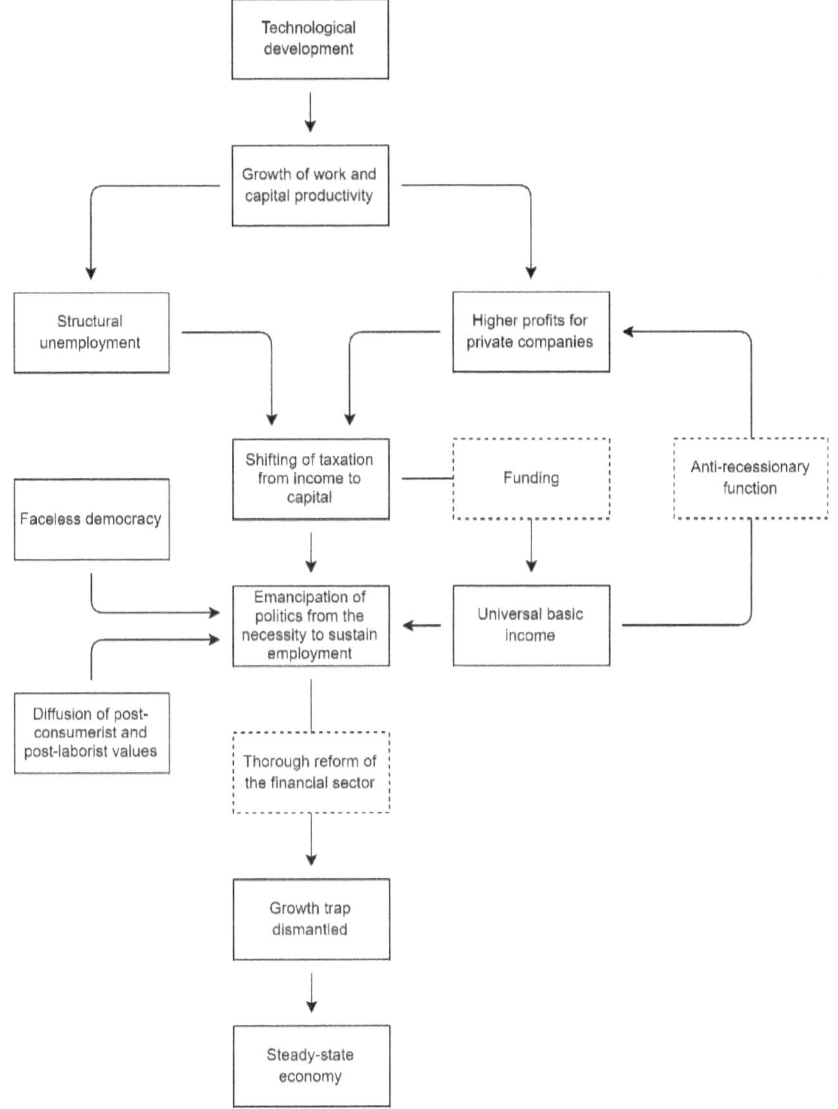

Transition

At the end of the 2050s, European political and institutional conditions were ripe for the birth of the first steady-state economies of modern history. However, the profound interdependencies among states in a globalized world would have made the transition of Europe alone to the new economic model unsustainable. In fact, under free market conditions, the commercial competition between isolated steady-state economies (bound to act within well-established ecological limits) and the old growth economies (who could ignore those limits with impunity) would have given the latter a significant edge. This was not due to their supposedly greater efficiency, but rather their practice of externalizing their own productive costs to ecosystems, effectively forcing future generations to pay for them. In such a scenario, capital flight towards the growth economies would have been inevitable and the new economic model in Europe would have been stillborn. That this situation was avoided was only thanks to a large amount of will for change by the international community, culminating in the establishment of the 'Global Sustainability Goals' in 2059: an internationally-negotiated, binding roadmap towards a sustainable world economy with no material growth. The agreement required each and every state to respect a tailored 'Ecological Impact Quota' (EIQ), which was established so that the sum of all quotas maintained the global ecological impact within long-term sustainable limits. The individual quotas, to be revised annually, were set according to a wide array of factors, of which population size and the energetic efficiency of the national economy were the two most important ones.

In order to fit within the limits of their EIQs, the over-developed economies initially had to undergo a process of degrowth. Although the diffusion of post-consumerist and post-laborist lifestyles among the population significantly facilitated this process,[121] it was ultimately only successfully implemented thanks to the profound regulatory and systemic reforms that reshaped the economic and productive structures of each individual country (in some cases, together with the implementation of population control policies; see Box 1). We will now briefly examine the key reforms:

---

121 See Chapter 7.

Regulatory reforms. The legislative measures adopted in the last few decades to counter the material growth of the economy are too many to mention here. Thus, we will simply concentrate on the four principal directions of the new legislation in Europe.

The first direction is comprised of a set of pre-emptive regulations which control the material and energetic input into the economy. These include:

1) A flexible taxation of basic commodities. The purpose of this is to discourage or incentivize the use of a commodity depending on its real-time ecological impact. If the aggregate impact from a commodity approaches the EIQ, taxation is increased.

2) The implementation of a license system for resource exploitation (both renewable and non-renewable). These licenses, limited in number, can be freely traded on the open market.[122]

The second direction of legislation entails new regulation of the productive sector inspired by the principles of efficiency and durability of both products and material capital. Among many measures, there are strict regulations on the use of packaging and transportation, a total prohibition on disposable products, and the criminalization of planned obsolescence.

The third direction involves long-term public investments that concentrate on green sectors, clean technologies and renewable energy generation.

The fourth and final direction comprises a stricter control on advertising and marketing. In this case the main regulatory tools were fiscal, with heavy taxation on all forms of advertising, and even heavier taxes on luxury products and sectors with a pronounced ecological impact.

Changes in the economic modes of production. The changes listed below came about as a consequence of the mutual reinforcement provided by the regulatory reforms described above, together with the spread of post-consumerist and post-laborist lifestyles. As a whole, they concern

---

122 This system resembles that adopted in some countries to control population size. See Box 1.

the diffusion of organizational and productive norms inspired by the principles of durability, environmental sustainability and energetic efficiency.

Box 1. Population control policies

In some countries, respecting the EIQ required the implementation of population control policies. It must be remembered that, according to the famous IPAT equation described in Chapter 2, population size constitutes one of the three main contributions to aggregate ecological impact, together with per capita consumption and the level of technological efficiency. Put simply, this means that 15 billion passionate ecologists, no matter how noble their intentions, will still tend to have a higher total impact than 5 billion reckless consumers. Fortunately, today a gradual decline in population no longer constitutes a grave problem for the economic system, in contrast to the late capitalist model. With fiscal systems decoupled from employment and public pensions abolished,[123] the pressure on the state to control the ratio between workers and the elderly vanished. As such, a decrease in population became not only ecologically desirable but also economically sustainable.

The numerous measures adopted by individual states to encourage a reduction in population include extensive public information campaigns to explain the link between demographic dimensions and ecological impact, economic incentives to adopt children rather than conceive them, and the introduction of a system of transferable procreation licenses. Due to the important role this last measure had (and continues to have) in counteracting demographic growth, and because of the ferocious historical debate fueled by their supposedly illiberal nature, the subject of procreation licenses deserves further attention here.

In states that implemented the procreation license system, each and every woman of fertile age is given a variable number of licenses (but typically one or two[124]), with each conferring the right to a biological son or daughter. If a woman wishes to have more children, she is free to buy additional licenses from other women who sell theirs freely. This effectively creates a free marketplace for births, where families with multiple children are automatically balanced by a corresponding number of couples without children, allowing for a controlled reduction of the population size.

---

123 See Chapter 3.

124 This number is selected to remain under the threshold of demographic replacement, which in advanced economies is currently slightly above two children per woman.

Compared to similar policies of the past, such as the well-known 'one-child policy' adopted by China at the end of the 20th century, the new system allows for a higher degree of flexibility for individuals, despite producing the same effect across the population. In case the desire to have children increases among the population as a whole, the price of procreation licenses grows according to the law of supply and demand, convincing more women – the least inclined to have more children of their own – to put theirs up for sale.

Most of the initial criticisms of this policy were centered on the possibility that the scheme could incentivize sales of procreation licenses motivated by situations of extreme poverty. Today, with UBI schemes as standard in all the advanced economies, the likelihood of this possibility is negligible, thus rendering the policy more ethically palatable. As such, in countries where the rationale behind this measure was explained to voters – again, made easier by the system of faceless democracy – the procreation license policy generally won the support of the population.

In the manufacturing sector, the old paradigm of 'creative destruction' was replaced with the idea of 'continuous improvement' as the main channel for material progress, leading to the development of practices aimed at creating easily-repaired and upgradable products. While in the past almost any leap in product quality corresponded with the release of a new model (be it a car, computer, television or electric razor), today improvement proceeds by the modification of existing products through the addition of better components, or the alteration of pre-existing ones. The result is a significant extension of the life-cycle of both material capital and products. The continual repair and improvement of all products entailed a decline in the production of brand-new objects and their corresponding aggregate ecological impact. At the same time, the repair sector grew exponentially, acquiring a size and economic importance without historical precedent. However, this change was not limited solely to the manufacturing sector. Today the construction industry concentrates on the restoration and energetic efficiency of existing buildings on the one hand, and the construction of new, durable buildings on the other. The agricultural sector takes much more interest in the integrity and preservation of the land that it uses. The transport sector focuses on local products and commodities, low-impact vehicles and short-distance routes. All sectors of the economy underwent similar shifts in parallel. The shift away from producing new things towards conserving what already exists also translated into a greater importance of services in the economy, creating new, qualified jobs in maintenance, repair and so on.

As a whole, the changes listed above significantly reduced the consumption of two macro-categories of goods:

1) The intrinsically superfluous goods and services that failed to contribute to human well-being, such as luxury cars, advertisements, single-use disposable objects and unnecessary gadgets.
2) Goods that serve a useful purpose but were historically consumed in quantities that far exceeded the optimal thresholds in terms of well-being,[125] or were thrown away before they became unusable. These included many consumer electronic devices (such as smartphones and laptops), clothes and personal vehicles.

By restoring the lost balance between the economy and the environment and curbing excess, the *degrowth* of GDP in over-developed countries produced a *growth* in aggregate well-being, to the surprise of many. It also served another crucial function: that of freeing up resources and ecological space for the development of the poorest countries, which could be then allowed to delay the transition to a steady-state economy until they had reached a more satisfactory level of material development, in terms of population well-being. However, there was a caveat – they were obliged to implement a progressive conversion of their economy towards ecological sustainability. This was to be achieved through an increase in the energetic efficiency of their economies and a reduction of the ecological impact of local production, among other means. In order to accelerate this conversion, the most developed economies offered technical and financial support at little or no cost.

In addition to signing binding international agreements, compliance was guaranteed by the introduction of new supranational rules regulating international trade, which implemented steep tariffs for the export and import of high-ecological-impact products. Today this impact is calculated based on the entire production-consumption chain, rather than measuring only the impact of upstream production, as was

---

125 See Chapter 1, Figures 1 and 2.

typical in the late capitalist era. Among the positive effects of the new regulations was a strong incentive for private companies to internalize their ecological costs, which added up to the numerous efforts in that direction set in motion by individual states, also agreed upon at the international level.

A new balance

During the 2080s, the 'Global Sustainability Goals' were finally achieved. For the first time since the industrial revolution, an absolute decoupling between GDP and matter occurred at the global level.[126] After the initial phase of degrowth drew to a close, Europe, together with most developed countries, became a steady-state economy. In this final section of the chapter we will analyze the main characteristics of this new model; however, before we begin, we must clarify two important points regarding its definition.

The first is rather obvious: a steady-state economy is something radically different from a growth economy in a phase of stagnation. As we have seen, for the latter the absence of growth represented the unwanted and unexpected result of a crisis. For a steady-state economy, on the other hand, it is the normal, healthy condition of the economic and productive system. The second clarification concerns the relationship between the economic system and the environment. Every human economy, regardless of its complexity, constitutes an open subsystem of a closed natural system – the planet Earth – characterized by scarce resources (in absolute terms) and fragile ecosystems. The economy draws in matter and energy at low levels of entropy, in the form of primary resources, and outputs high-entropy matter and energy in the form of pollution and waste. The second principle of thermodynamics ensures that this reality is unavoidable, and applies equally to the now-defunct growth economies and modern steady-state economies. The difference lies in the way they relate to this reality. Growth economies operated under the assumption of an imaginary separation between the economic and natural systems, essentially rejecting their intimate relationship. On the contrary, steady-state economies base their structural features and long-term objectives on

---

126 See Chapter 2, section 'On the brink of ecological disaster'.

that very relationship. It follows that the modern concept of a 'steady-state economy' requires the semantic and theoretical boundaries erected by traditional economics to be torn down. Just as it is not possible to speak of biology without referencing chemistry, today it is impossible to speak of economics without referencing ecology.

Having clarified these points, we can move on to define a 'steady-state' economy as one in which the total flow of high-entropy matter and energy – that is, not reusable by humans – generated throughout the entire cycle of production and consumption remains stable at a given level in the long term.[127] Whereas a growth economy is unsustainable by definition, the sustainability of a steady-state economy depends on how high this level is set. We can thus consider a steady-state economy to be sustainable when:

- The aggregate use of renewable resources does not surpass the capacities of ecosystems to regenerate them;
- The rate of depletion of non-renewable resources is lower than the rate of development of renewable substitutes;
- The generation of waste and pollution is below the capacity of ecosystems to reabsorb and dispose of them.[128]

The initial degrowth of the over-developed economies was fundamental to satisfying these criteria. The regulatory, economic, productive and cultural changes discussed up until now which made degrowth possible are to a large extent the same changes that now allow modern steady-state economies to maintain long-term sustainability.

However, a fundamental question remains to be answered: what does the economic cycle look like in the absence of growth? At the beginning of this chapter, we explained that the far-reaching reform of the financial system managed to dismantle the growth trap, but what are the characteristics of the new system that succeeded it? Since a comprehensive answer would require a separate volume, we will limit ourselves to touching briefly on a few fundamental points.

---

127 Short-term fluctuations within certain limits are certainly possible. This means that in a steady-state economy, GDP can grow without compromising the sustainability of the system, so long as aggregate material input and throughput remain constant. Unlike in the defunct growth economies, however, the growth of GDP is not a necessary condition for the stability of the system.

128 These three principles were first enunciated more than a century ago in Daly, H.E. *Towards a steady-state economy*, W.H. Freeman & Co, 1973.

As we have already mentioned, the disappearance of the ancient means of monetary expansion made any high-risk speculation that was not supported by real money[129] particularly difficult. The consequence of this was that more and more capital returned to the material economy, settling on safe, long-term investments. As an effect of the cultural, regulatory, economic and productive changes discussed up until now, these investments are now largely centered on the maintenance and improvement of existing goods, rather than their continuous substitution, as was the case in the past. The constant growth in the quality of material capital and products translates into a continuous increase in their economic value, keeping investments (and loans) potentially profitable. The qualitative growth of the economy, supported by time preferences that are still positive[130] – albeit lower than they once were due to the spread of post-consumerist lifestyles – also keeps interest rates above zero, allowing the credit system to function smoothly despite the constant size of the economy.

With monetary intervention now reserved for exceptional cases, stable material capital and production have produced an economic system that naturally fluctuates between moderate inflation and moderate deflation. As the total money available in markets is now kept largely constant, when production increases too much the economy enters a phase of deflation. While this represented a tragedy in a system based on maximizing GDP and employment,[131] it is entirely normal within the modern steady-state and post-laborist economies. Simply put, falling prices incentivize savings and reduce purchases.[132] Increased savings translate into lower interest rates on loans offered by banks, which incentivize companies to invest. Over time, the contraction of production pushes up prices, leading the economy into a new inflationary phase. This stimulates a rise in purchasing and a consequent recovery of economic activity. Meanwhile, the safety net constituted by the UBI forestalls the possibility of recession,[133] thus dampening the peaks of an already moderate economic cycle.[134]

---

129 As opposed to the fictitious money which coursed through the late capitalist financial sector.

130 In economics, positive time preferences mean that with the value of goods held constant, individuals generally prefer to use them sooner rather than later.

131 See Chapter 2, section *'Credit, monetary expansion and the economic cycle'*.

132 In the old growth economies, purchasing was labelled as 'consumer spending'.

133 Of course, recessions can still be triggered by unforeseen external events, such as wars, pandemics etc.

134 See Chapter 6, section *'The growth trap dismantled'*.

7 LIFE AT THE TURN OF THE 22nd CENTURY

Having reviewed the overarching structural changes that followed the collapse of the late capitalist system, we will now examine the main social and cultural factors associated with those changes, both causal and consequential.

Needless to say, the modern steady-state economies did not emerge in a sociocultural vacuum, nor could they have survived in one for very long. They are not clockwork organizations, but rather human institutions, and as such their existence is grounded in the human beings who make them possible. Not ordinary human beings, however, but human beings who have succeeded in breaking free from the chains of excessive work and consumption; who have been able to delegate the role of driving the economy to technological, organizational and material capital; and who decided to dedicate themselves to the pursuit of a decommodified and substantive well-being.

A thorough exploration of this new model of individual and the society in which he lives is beyond the scope of this chapter,[135] which instead assumes a humbler focus on three key aspects of the transition from the late capitalist civilization to the contemporary one. In the order in which they are discussed, these are:

- The shift from a culture of consumption to a culture of use;
- The shift from a laborist economy to a deliberative economy;
- The shift from a core-periphery territorial model to a diffuse, multipolar spatial configuration.

From a culture of consumption to a culture of use

Ours is no longer a consumerist society, in the sense that consumption does not constitute the core of economic, social and personal life.

---

135 For those interested in learning more about this topic, a good starting point is F. Boeri's essay, *The return of the Renaissance man*, Craveri, 2094.

What does this mean in practice? First of all, it means that the elimination of planned obsolescence and the consequent extension of the lifetime of products went hand in hand with a substantial reduction in the 'psychological obsolescence' related to what we earlier designated 'the cult of novelty'. This was a direct result of the modification of lifestyles that accompanied the great social, economic and institutional transformations of the last 60 years. The decline of both planned and psychological obsolescence deeply altered the way in which people related to material products, thus reshaping the very idea of consumption. Whereas at the beginning of the century most material products that were available for purchase on the market were considered 'consumer goods', this expression currently describes only products that are *inherently* perishable, namely whose usage entails their destruction or irreversible transformation. Under this new definition food, beverage, cosmetics, cigars and ink are all categorized as consumer goods. In turn, unlike in the past, products such as clothes, razors, computers, smartphones and cutlery fall outside of this category, instead classified as 'usage goods'. Usage goods are those whose use does not compromise their function, and which can thus be constantly repaired and modified, extending their life cycle indefinitely.

It bears repeating,[136] however, that psychological obsolescence was not the only cultural factor that encouraged over-consumption in late capitalist societies. In addition, there was a close association of consumption with social status, which was fueled and perpetuated by social imitation and a deeply materialist mass culture. As we have seen, this association played a key role in propping up an economic system based on perpetual and endless growth. Such a role, already undermined at a cultural level by the collapse of the late capitalist system and the subsequent social and institutional changes (primarily the Universal Basic Income), became structurally superfluous with the dismantlement of the growth trap.

Hence, the second half of the 21st century bore witness to a progressive dematerialization of social status, which went hand in hand with its emancipation from work and career. Although one can still pursue happiness in the acquisition of private yachts and jets – assuming a willingness to comply with the heavy taxation on goods with a high ecological impact – their owner is no longer automatically granted access to the circle of 'successful' people. On the contrary, they

---

are exposed to blame and social disapproval. Unfortunately for those devoted to excess, 'to keep the economy rolling' has ceased to serve as a valid justification for ecological irresponsibility, and the same can be said for the creation of pointless jobs.

The dissociation of consumption and social status, alongside the emergence of a culture of use, has had profound effects on society's aggregate ecological impact. This can be illustrated with the example of the transport sector. If we measure value in terms of usage (in this case mobility), rather than in terms of products (in this case means of transport), there is no difference between a car that provides mobility for twenty years and two cars that provide ten years of mobility each. Although the usage value is the same, in the case of a single car the productive and ecological costs are halved. For this reason, today everyone would consider the durable car the better option, given that with the same benefits, a lower cost is preferable. In the late capitalist era, however, the same logic would have led most people to prefer two cars over one. This was not only for the evident support this afforded to the economic system in terms of jobs and growth, but also because of the way in which a consumerist culture regarded products as vehicles of status, attributing to them an intrinsic value independent of their use and inversely proportional to their age. As such, to own two brand new cars granted more social prestige, regardless of whether they were actually used or simply left parked in a garage. Thus the higher ecological impact generated by the production of one additional car – or one thousand, or ten thousand – appeared to be the price that had to be paid for the preferable option (two cars), when in reality it was an additional cost to pay for the worst case.

With the decline of both commodified status and the once widespread compulsion towards novelty, today it is mainly the utility of the *performance* associated with a product that leads people to purchase it. Here I define the 'performance' of a product, according to modern usage in sociology,[137] as the practical execution of its functionality in a specific context of use. If the functionality of a product defines what it can potentially do, its performance describes the usage that is actually derived from it. Although its functionality is unchanged, the performance of a car that can accelerate to 180 mph is different in a country with a maximum speed limit of 90 mph, when compared to a country without maximum speed restrictions. Similarly, the

---

137 For instance, see Bloomer, 2088.

performance of a domestic robot is merely to vacuum dust if this is all that it is used for, regardless of the hundreds of additional tasks it may be capable of (i.e. its functionality).

It should be noted that a product's performance tends to decline with the acquisition of multiple units. Using two combs instead of one does not improve one's hairstyle, just as using two umbrellas instead of one does not keep a person drier. Attributing value to the performance of a product, rather than its functionality, means limiting purchases to objects that have clear usage value. It means owning only one umbrella and one comb, and giving them away if they are not used.

To quote the philosopher Enrico Fode, "Today we purchase performance, rather than products. Value once seemed to spring out of possessing things – musical instruments, a state-of-the-art kitchen, luxury furniture or a home gym. Now it emerges from the possibilities afforded by those things – to make music, enjoy a meal, to rest comfortably and to safeguard one's health."[138] The principle of *efficiency* in the process of production (exemplified by the elimination of planned obsolescence and the continual upgrading of products) has been complemented by the principle of *sufficiency* at the point of usage, whereby people limit their acquisition of objects to those needed for the performance they intend to exploit.

Active well-being and the deliberative economy

The demise of the cult of growth and production, the advent of the modern culture of use and the introduction of the UBI have collectively put an end to the traditional division of life between work and consumption, time-as-a-commodity (to be sold for a salary) and time-as-a-container (to be filled to the brim with entertainment).

The passive leisure of the late capitalist era has to a large extent been supplanted by an active leisure involving arts and crafts, study, political activism, personal development, volunteering, subsistence agriculture, exploring and caring for the local heritage, and so on. This decommodified leisure, while not contributing to GDP, increases aggregate well-being and reduces our impact on the environment. Likewise, the dementedly hurried, intrinsically superfluous work of the

---

138 Fode, E. *The past consumed*, self-published, 2093, p. 97.

early 21st century has given way to vocational activities motivated by passion and curiosity rather than profit and status – or, even worse, by an irrational sense of duty. Unnecessary production and activity are no longer considered virtues regardless of external considerations. Today, one asks oneself: what is it that I am producing? What is this activity in which I am engaged? Needless to say, to produce weapons or electronic trinkets does not contribute to the well-being of society as a whole, whether or not a demand exists for those products.

Together, vocational work and active leisure defined the historical transition from a laborist economy to what has recently been termed a 'deliberative economy'.[139] The latter is propelled by an education system that instils autonomy, critical thinking and a joy in learning, making the natural emergence of the interests and talents of each person possible. The financial security provided by the UBI grants everyone the privilege of developing those interests and talents, potentially transforming them – for those who so desire – into professional activities.

This new economic model has not eliminated competition, but it has blunted its edges. While merit is still rewarded, those who fall behind in the career competition are not excluded, obliged to renounce their dreams or forced to sell themselves in order to stay afloat. On the contrary, those who do not satisfy the standards of the market are offered the possibility to continue to pursue their passions while living with less, or to take the time needed to cultivate their talents.

Naturally, some people choose to live with only the UBI and dedicate all their time to activities that fall outside of the market economy. These people, owing to their limited financial resources, tend to have a lower-than-average ecological impact, supporting the environmental sustainability of the system. However, most prefer to complement their activities outside the market (active leisure) with one or more working activities. As material production is largely automated and the useless jobs that thrived on over-production and over-consumption have disappeared, today's work is concentrated in services, culture, science and art. Alongside those who perform more traditional professions, such as cooks, physicians, lawyers or

---

139 Martinez, L. *The emergence of the deliberative economy*, Senesi, 2092. The expression 'vocational economy', preferred by some commentators, is inadequate as it excludes human activities mainly motivated by economic gain. These human activities, as we saw in Chapter 3, include the most exhausting and tedious jobs, which cannot be considered a vocation but are among the best paid, and are thus performed by those who tend to value money over time.

firefighters, the modern deliberative economies are characterized by an unprecedented number of artists, engineers, scientists and researchers. Their work is predominantly autonomous or semi-autonomous, either through self-employment or participation in horizontally-organized networks linked to single projects.

Regardless of their profession, people generally spend only a small fraction of their time working, so much so that their activities would have been considered part-time a century ago. Despite the small number of hours dedicated to their jobs, the high intrinsic motivation of today's workers results in an average productivity that is very close to that of workers in the late capitalist era, who often spent eight or more hours working per day.

The emancipation from work provided by the UBI also had positive effects on the quality of information in society. This is not only because those who watch or read the news have more time to filter and analyze the information they receive, but also because journalists – the vast majority of whom are now independent – are finally allowed to dedicate themselves to thorough research and thoughtful communication of the news, without the risk of ending up in the street. Likewise, scientists and scholars, particularly in the humanities and social sciences, can now afford to carry out independent research. These people have been liberated from ties to any particular institution, but are in constant contact with a new deinstitutionalized, non-hierarchical academic world organized as a fluid network of individuals and informal groups.[140]

However, the most surprising effect of freeing up much of humanity's time from work and consumption was undoubtedly the awakening of a community spirit that had long been inhibited by the social hegemony of the state and the market. Today, this community spirit is embodied by burgeoning grassroots networks of free citizens cooperating for the common good. This is not the semblance of cooperation presented by the late capitalist NGOs, which were often more interested in acquiring prestige for their management and securing public funds than in furthering the noble causes they espoused. Rather, it is the genuine cooperation that emerges from an authentic civil society made up of individuals that choose to organize informally to serve their community, or simply socialize and shape their

---

140 Their work is easier still, thanks to the internationally-agreed deregulation of copyright that took place in the 2060s, which made access to scientific publications free for all.

common future. Among them are people who clean rivers and parks, organize free lessons in various disciplines (from yoga to DIY, from music to gardening), offer guided tours of the local vicinity, repair clothes or electronics, and even those who teach others how to do the same. Given the sheer number and variety of the activities that this new multipolar and horizontal community activism entails, providing a comprehensive list would be impossible.[141]

Curiously enough, although the scale of this voluntary cooperation appeared utopian when viewed through a lens tinted by traditional economic thinking, today it is a plainly evident reality. This fact demonstrates how the compulsory sharing enforced by old socialist regimes, which subsumed the individual into the collective, was not the only feasible alternative to the late capitalist model's elevation of egoism as a virtue. As we have discovered in the last 50 years, social reality is not beholden to Karl Marx or Ayn Rand. It is not a two-dimensional continuum between two contrasting hells. A third way exists, in which we are living right now. It is an outrageous utopia with less work, less consumption and more well-being. A new well-being – or perhaps just one that was forgotten for a time – liberated from the glistening facades of shopping malls, from the gaudy and hypnotic greyness of mindless consumerism. A decommodified and genuine well-being that does not hinge on differences between the self and the other, or the comparison between richer and poorer, but rather finds new heights in sharing. A well-being that arises from the satisfaction of something created, of something done, of an experience lived, of a friendship forged, of an idea made reality, of a common project. A well-being that our ancestors vainly sought through a commodified status whose frantic pursuit took the guise of material accumulation and purposeless growth. A well-being that today is realized in the harmony that springs forth from sufficiency, in deliberate cooperation, in the free and self-determined development of everyone's talents and passions.

The land beyond the economy

---

141 This is not to say that some people have not tried. For example, see Li, X. *Civil society deconstructed: characteristics and functions of the new autonomous volunteering*, Blue Mantle Editions, 2085.

Having shed the role of producer-consumer, human beings have been able to slowly rebuild a new, non-predatory balance with their physical environment. Whereas land in the late capitalist era was reduced to a mere *space* for the deployment of economic functions (the shopping mall, the holiday resort, the industrial suburb), today it is first and foremost a *place* with intrinsic value to protect and relate to from an ecosystemic perspective. This value is not only measured in economic and material terms, but rather in terms of livability and well-being, keeping in mind that the latter criteria are not always compatible with the former.

Of course, rebuilding the intrinsic value of lands that had long been pillaged by the market could not be achieved overnight. Rather, it was the outcome of a coordinated, collaborative project over several decades,[142] in which local and national institutions, civil society and residents played a central role. On a concrete level, the project had several goals. It was about the widespread implementation of reforestation and the restoration of biodiversity, both of flora and fauna. It was about redeeming the peri-urban plains, returning their rolling monocultured fields to a more traditional and sustainable model of agriculture, inspired by ethical criteria and supported by a locally-minded and ecologically-aware market. It was about identifying paths towards the restoration of the ecosystems that had been compromised by overexploitation and the commodification of land. Meanwhile, on a symbolic level, the project was about initiating the rediscovery of the local architectural, cultural and artistic peculiarities. It was about eliminating the cloying structures that packaged entire buildings, neighborhoods and cities like museums for tourist consumption, and handing those places back to their resident communities. It was about dampening the destructive and homogenizing frenzy of mass tourism, which systematically drained places of identity only to transform them into enormous theme parks, to instead substitute it with the slow pleasure of travel and of living one's locality.

This process was facilitated by the spread of self-employment, the progressive digitalization of intellectual work and a swelling disenchantment with the frantic lifestyles of the large cities. This triggered a reverse migration back towards mountain areas and the countryside during the second half of the 21st century. The largest cities saw their population reduced, and with it their economic prominence,

---

142 To be more precise, a multitude of projects inspired by a common vision.

generating a crisis for the old core-periphery model, in tandem with the other great societal changes discussed in previous chapters. The centralizing and predatory metropoles of a century ago, which voraciously consumed lands near and far with unbridled gluttony, have ceded to a complex territorial configuration composed of independent small towns and villages connected via trade and mutual aid into ecologically sustainable macro-regions, in which the cycles of water, food, waste and (where possible) energy are contained and self-sufficient. The result is a non-hierarchical and multipolar network of towns and villages spread across the plains, valleys, coasts and mountains, each in a symbiotic balance with its surroundings and characterized by low-impact, locally-sourced consumption. Around each node in the network are interconnected green belts that make the traditional functional segregation of rural land into transit zones, natural parks, tourist areas and vast agricultural zones a thing of the past. In their place are anthropized but thriving ecosystems in which the preservation of diversity of habitats such as woods, rivers, lakes, plains and mountains fuses with sustainable agriculture, the conservation of hydrogeological assets, onsite waste treatment and renewable energy production.[143] Together, these green belts constitute a geographical limit, in addition to the economic and material limits imposed by Ecological Impact Quotas,[144] beyond which urban development must not extend. It is a self-imposed limit that follows from the rejection of material growth as a social goal, as well as from a widespread consciousness of the well-being that this rejection has brought, and continues to bring, to the population.

Within cities, the digitalization of work and the spread of self-employment called into question the age-old division of residential areas from working areas. The phenomenon of commuting, an aberrant consequence of the core-periphery territorial model, is today a distant memory, as an increasing proportion of human activity is conducted from home or, more often, in shared spaces distributed liberally throughout the urban territory. These atelier-offices are open to all, where people engage in professional activities or develop active leisure projects, individually or in collaboration with others. They are workshops of ideas and relationships based on the sharing of interests

---

143 In such a context, the modern super-automated industrial areas are strategically located in order to minimize interference with human life and ecosystems.

144 See Chapter 6.

and passions, in which to build horizontal professional and social links either by rubbing shoulders with those present or – thanks to modern virtual reality technologies – with people on the other side of the world.

The dematerialization of work, the rediscovery of the joy of residing somewhere and the sustainable relocation of production and consumption cycles[145] led to a reduced movement of people and goods, with tangible benefits not only for the environment but also on the structure of urban areas. Most of the old ways of traversing the urban sprawl have been abandoned, and cities today are crossed on foot, by bike, with small individual electric vehicles (such as hoverboards or electric scooters), or by making use of a highly efficient public transport network. Of course, cars still exist, but their use has been limited to the territory outside the cities. Convenient car parks are located in the outskirts of every town and village, where people leave their private vehicles in order to continue to travel on the public transport networks that connect them to the urban interior. However, for longer journeys most people prefer electric trains and buses, due to their higher efficiency and lower costs.

Aside from dramatically reducing pollution, excluding cars from cities has eased the ubiquitous traffic of the late capitalist era, making travel easier and faster. Public vehicles (for human transport) and private vans (purely for the transport of goods) hurtle along the main arteries of the city, while within neighborhoods the streets have been replaced with verdant lawns and lush trees, under which children and adults can move freely without fear of being struck down by a speeding car or choked by pollution. Bicycles and small electric vehicles course along dedicated lanes that run parallel to the green pedestrian areas, while respecting their limits.

Against all odds, after centuries of indiscriminate exploitation, the land has returned to being a cradle of life, a home, and a shelter. Against all odds, the producer-consumer has returned to being a resident.

---

145 This included the local completion of food, water, waste and energy chains.

CONCLUSION

We have in due course arrived at the end of our journey through the great upheavals that have characterized this tumultuous century. Before we take our leave, I think it would be wise to reacquaint ourselves with the major milestones we have passed along the way.

The late capitalist age. In Part one, we explored the deep structure of the late capitalist system and the complex relationships that intimately linked its culture, institutions, economic model and social dynamics. We saw how this system depended on constant economic growth to maintain stable levels of employment and counterbalance the inflationary pressure exerted by constant monetary expansion. A wealth of empirical evidence demonstrated there was almost no correlation between economic growth and human well-being beyond a specific threshold of wealth. Despite this, the dominant economic discourse, aided and abetted by the twin ethics of work and consumption, perpetuated the illusion of a linear relationship between growth and well-being, affording the system philosophical and cultural legitimacy. This legitimacy was to crumble after the turn of the millennium, when unprecedented environmental challenges, coupled with the structural unemployment wrought by the progressive automation of the economy, exposed the broad structural limits of this economic and cultural model for all to see. Nonetheless, the world was to wait many long years before a widespread recognition of these limits could translate into concrete action; years during which politicians proved utterly incapable of making wise choices, hostage to ferocious populist trends and paralyzed by a seemingly unsolvable dichotomy between protection of the environment and economic stability.

The three revolutions. In Part two we saw how, when all seemed lost, change finally emerged in the form of three ground-breaking revolutions: a revolution in the redistribution of wealth, a revolution in the education system, and a revolution in politics and governance. Each was simultaneously both the cause and effect of the spread of post-laborist and post-consumerist values to increasingly broad swathes of the population. The shift from a hierarchical, externally-imposed model of education to one that was horizontal and self-directed shattered the core element of the socialization process by which young people in the late capitalist era were molded into compulsive consumers, obedient workers and passive voters. The transformation of the old stage democracies into full-fledged faceless democracies brought about a shift from an emotion-based politics to a reason-based politics, liberating the political arena from the threat of populism. Finally, the suppression of the ancient systems of selective welfare in the wake of the introduction of a pan-European UBI transformed work from an economic necessity into an individual vocation.

The dawn of a new civilization. In the third and final part of the book, we described the role of the three revolutions in the process of first dismantling the growth trap and then radically reforming the existing economic and financial systems. Within just a few years, these reforms managed to bring about a transition from old growth economies to modern steady-state economies. The many environmental problems wrought by the late capitalist system could thus be solved, and a new balance could be reached between human society and global ecosystems. We then explored the shift from a culture of consumption to a culture of use, and the economic transition from a laborist economy to a deliberative economy, in which vocational activities and active leisure supplanted superfluous work and passive consumption. Finally, we highlighted one of the most ironic turns of events of recent years: the transformation of some of the greatest problems that tormented our ancestors into the very foundations of the prosperity and well-being that we enjoy today. Indeed, the absence of growth of the material economy, low levels of consumption, and above all technological innovation, morphed from being terrifying threats into the key elements of current prosperity.

Far from marking the end of history, solving the arduous, multifaceted crisis that humanity faced was actually the precondition for history to continue. What we did saved us from an ecological and social suicide that once seemed inevitable. Nonetheless, much work remains to be done. The gap between nations in terms of well-being, although substantially narrowed, has not yet been fully closed, and some countries have yet to feel the benefits of the century's historic economic and social reforms. While this gap persists, the implementation of a global universal basic income will remain out of reach.[146]

As for the environment, ecosystems damaged by centuries of over-exploitation are recovering their fragile equilibria thanks to huge efforts at restoration over the past few decades. However, the road remains fraught with obstacles, and unforeseeable events may place these accomplishments in jeopardy. Many terrestrial ecosystems were also damaged beyond the point of recovery, and will thus remain as lasting reminders of the destruction that human excess can wreak.

My generation witnessed the collapse of a civilization that it was believed would be eternal, as well as the dawn of another that was believed to be impossible. As I write I am 78 years old, and I can confidently state that the world of today is a better place than the one into which I was born. In all likelihood, many decades must pass before we see whether the progress made in this century is destined to last; if humanity has really matured, as I hope is the case, or if instead our era represents nothing but a rare and ephemeral spark of good sense in a history dominated by folly and excess. What is certain is that our current civilization has provided humanity the means with which to build itself a future. Perhaps it will be a prosperous future that sees us reach the stars, or perhaps the forces of egoism and greed will re-emerge and drag humanity back into the swamp. As for me, I think there are good reasons to look forward to the future with optimism. If nothing else because, unlike a century ago, we can at least say with confidence that there will be one.

---

146 Fortunately, some positive progress has been made in this regard, and the recent agreements forged in Chisinau create hope for the future. See Cagliati, M. *The Chisinau pact in the framework of a global UBI*, Aspi Insitute Report, April 2096, pp. 73-98.

BIBLIOGRAPHY

An economy for the 99%, Oxfam, 2017.

Becker, F. A *brief history of human well-being*, Ocean Press, 2092.

Blanchflower, D. G., Oswald, A. J. *Well-being over time in Britain and the USA*, in "Journal of Public Economics", 88 (2004), pp. 1359-1386.

Bloomer, J. *Microsociology for a post-consumerist society*, Phoenix Press, 2088.

Boeri, F. *The return of the Renaissance man*, Craveri, 2094.

Brunori, P., Ferreira, F., Peragine, V. *Inequality of opportunity, income inequality and economic mobility: some international comparisons*, Policy Research working paper n. WPS 6304, World Bank, 2013.

Brynjolfsson, E., McAfee, A. *Race against the machine: how the digital revolution is accelerating innovation, driving productivity, and irreversibly transforming employment and the economy*, Digital Frontier Press, 2011.

Cagliati, M. *The Chisinau pact in the framework of a global UBI*, Aspi Insitute Report, April 2096, pp. 73-98.

Cooper, J. *Manual of historical sociology*, Duranti, 2088.

Csikszentmihalyi, M. *Materialism and the evolution of consciousness*, in T. Kasser, A. D. Kanner (a cura di), *Psychology and consumer culture: the struggle for a good life in a materialistic world*, APA Books, 2004.
(DOI: 91-106. 10.1037/10658-006)

D'Addio, A. C. *Intergenerational transmission of disadvantage: mobility or immobility across generations? A review of the evidence for OECD countries*, OECD Publishing, 2007 ("OECD Social, Employment and Migration Working Papers", 52).

Daly, H. E. *The steady state economy*, W.H. Freeman & Co. Ltd Ed, 1972.

Daly, H. E. *Toward a steady-state economy*, W.H. Freeman & Co., 1973.

Daly, H. E. *A steady-state economy*, Sustainable Development Commission (UK), 2008.

Daly, H. E., *Three limits to growth*, University of Maryland, School of Public Policy, 2014 (https://ourworld.unu.edu/en/three-limits-to-growth).

De Masi, S. *Lavorare gratis, lavorare tutti. Perché il futuro è dei disoccupati*, Rizzoli, 2017.

Di Tella, R., MacCulloch, R. *Happiness adaptation to income beyond 'basic needs'.* In E. Diener, J. Helliwell, D. Kahneman, *International differences in well-being*, Oxford University Press, 2010.

Donati, E. *Time and knowledge in the 21st century*, self-published, 2093.

Ermisch, J., Jäntti, M., Smeeding, T. *From parents to children: the intergenerational transmission of advantage*, Russell Sage Foundation, 2012.

Fode, E. *Memories of a forgotten past*, Redbridge, 2089.

Fode, E. *The past consumed*, self-published, 2093.

Foglia, A. *Towards a politics of reason*, Plans Trivium Press, 2069.

Frey, C. B., Osborne, M. *Technology at work. The future of innovation and employment*, University of Oxford, 2015.

Gallino, L. *Finanzcapitalismo*, Einaudi, 2011.

Guidolin, M., La Jeunesse, E. A. *The decline in the U.S. personal saving rate: is it real and is it a puzzle?* Federal Reserve Bank of St. Louis Review, 6:89(2007), pp. 491–514.
(DOI: 10.20955/r.89.491-514)

Happy Planet Index report, New Economics Foundation (NEF), 2017.

Huesemann, M. H., Huesemann, J. A. *Technofix: why technology won't save us or the environment*, New Society Publishers, 2011.

Human Development Report 2006, UNDP, 2006.

Human Development Report 2016, UNDP, 2016.

Human Development Report 2017, UNDP, 2017.

Illich, I. *Tools for conviviality*, Marion Boyars Publishers, 1973.

Illich, I. *Energy and equity*, Harper & Row, 1974.

Inglehart, R., Foa, R., Peterson, C., Welzel, C. *Development, freedom, and rising happiness: a global perspective (1981–2007)*, in "Perspectives on Psychological Science", 3:4 (2008), pp. 264– 285.
(DOI: 10.1111/j.1745-6924.2008.00078.x)

International Energy Outlook 2017, US Energy Information Administration (EIA), 2017.

International Monetary Fund: http://www.imf.org/external/index.htm

Jackson, T. *Prosperity without growth: foundations for the economy of tomorrow*, Routledge, 2017.

Kahneman, D., Deaton, A. *High income improves evaluation of life but not emotional well-being*, in "Proceedings of the National Academy of Sciences of the United States of America", 107:38 (2010), pp. 16489-93.
(DOI: 10.1073/pnas.1011492107.2010)

Karagiannaki, E. *The effect of parental wealth on children's outcomes in early adulthood*, in "Journal of Economic Inequalities", 15 (2017), pp. 217–243.
(DOI: 10.1007/s10888-017-9350-1)

Kasser, T. *Values and prosperity*, Sustainable development commission (UK), 2007.

Latouche, S. *L'invention de l'économie*, Albin Michel, 2005.

Layard, R., Nickell, S., Mayraz, G. *The marginal utility of income*, in "Journal of Public Economics", 92:8/9 (2008), pp. 1846-1857.

Li, X. *Civil society deconstructed: characteristics and functions of the new autonomous volunteering*, Blue Mantle Editions, 2085.

Long, S. *Faceless democracy. A new model for Europe*, Exen Press, 2061.

Magnaghi, A. *Il progetto locale. Verso la coscienza di luogo*, Bollati Boringhieri, 2010.

Martinez, L. *The emergence of the deliberative economy*, Senesi, 2092.

Matveev, V. *Elements for a post-capitalist sociology*, Merriam Publications, 2091.

McLuhan, M. *Understanding media: the extensions of man*, Signet Books, 1966.

Mischel, L., Davis, A. *CEO pay continues to rise as typical workers are paid less*, issue brief n. 380, Economic Policy Institute, 2014. (https://www.epi.org/files/2014/ceo-pay-continues-to-rise.pdf)

Morel, E. *The second short century*, Cassio, 2087.

Moretti, E. *Experiential learning. A toolkit for young researchers and explorers*, self-published, 2095.

National Footprint Accounts 2016, Global Footprint Network, 2016.

Nemecek, T., Jungbluth, N., Milà i Canals, L., Schenck, R. *Environmental impacts of food consumption and nutrition: where are we and what is next?*, in "International journal of Life Cycle Assessment", 21 (2016), pp. 607-620.
(DOI: 10.1007/s11367-016-1071-3)

William of Ockham, *Summa Totius Logicae*, I. 12, 1323.

OECD, *Basic income as a policy option: can it add up?* Report, May 2017.

OSCE: https://www.osce.org

Oxfam Briefing Paper, Oxfam, January 2017.

Perrin, A. *A political history of Europe*, Acropolis, 2078.

Pickett, K. E., Wilkinson, R. G. *Income inequality and health: a causal review.* In "Social Science & Medicine", 128 (2015), pp. 316-326. (DOI: https://doi.org/10.1016/j.socscimed.2014.12.031)

Proto, E., Rustichini, A. *A reassessment of the relationship between GDP and life satisfaction*, in "PLoS ONE", 8 (2013). (DOI: 8:11.https://doi.org/10.1371/journal.pone.0079358)

Proto, E., Rustichini, A. *GDP and life satisfaction: new evidence*, 2014 (https://voxeu.org/article/gdp-and-life-satisfaction-new-evidence).

Reeves, A. *Mediacracy: rise and decline of a political model*, self-published, 2086.

Sella, F. *Autonomy and responsibility of students in contemporary education*, Carmeli, 2096.

Serfati, C. *The current financial meltdown: a Crisis of finance capital-driven globalization*, University of London, 2009.

State of the World 2004, Worldwatch institute, 2004.

State of the World 2008, Worldwatch institute, 2008.

The Conference Board Total Economy Database: http://www.conference-board.org/data/economydatabase/

Volkov, S. *The red steppes*, Chrono, 2050.

Wilson, E. O. *The diversity of life*, Penguin Press, 2001.

World Bank: http://www.worldbank.org

Zinn, H. *A people's history of the United States*, Harper Perennial, 2005.